P9-AQU-774

808.51   131183
T73s

DATE DUE			

WITHDRAWN

Stagefright

Letting It Work for You

Robert Triplett

CARL A. RUDISILL LIBRARY
LENOIR RHYNE COLLEGE

NELSON-HALL *nh* CHICAGO

808.51
T73s
131183
Mar.1985

Line drawings by Cea Corb

LIBRARY OF CONGRESS CATALOGING IN PUBLICATION DATA

Triplett, Robert.
 Stagefright.

 Includes index.
 1. Stage fright.   I. Title.
PN2071.P78T74   1983   808.5'1   82-14205
ISBN 0-88229-720-1

Copyright © 1983 by Robert Triplett

Reprinted 1984

All rights reserved. No part of this book may be reproduced in any form without permission in writing from the publisher, except by a reviewer who wishes to quote brief passages in connection with a review written for broadcast or for inclusion in a magazine or newspaper. For information address Nelson-Hall, Inc., Publishers, 111 North Canal Street, Chicago, Illinois 60606.

Manufactured in the United States of America

10 9 8 7 6 5 4 3 2

The paper in this book is pH neutral (acid-free).

CONTENTS

INTRODUCTION

IN A SURVEY BY THE *Times* of London, October 7, 1973, some three thousand inhabitants of the United States were asked, "What are you most afraid of?" Almost half (41 percent) responded, "Speaking before a group," and thereby placed stagefright at the top of the list. It outranked by a large margin other fears such as the threat of sickness, financial problems, even death.

Since stagefright causes anxiety for so many, this book is written for a wide audience. Although it focuses on a broad spectrum of professional performers—speakers, musicians, athletes, actors, dancers—its message speaks to performers in the widest context: lawyers addressing the court, housewives leading club programs, executives facing difficult board meetings, salespersons presenting new products.

Most persons try to overcome or camouflage stagefright by trying to rigidly control their thoughts and feelings. The thesis of this book is that by accepting stagefright rather than by seeking to control it, nervous tensions can be changed into productive energy and transformed into a sense of assurance.

The book is divided into two major sections. Part I, The Process, explains the way stagefright is experienced by performers, and presents a working hypothesis of the way in which it is transformed. Part II, The Practice, spells out a number of techniques that will aid the performer in the transformation process.

In addition the Appendix brings out important correlations between stagefright and nutrition.

Many readers will be aware of my debt to several great thinkers of the twentieth century: C. G. Jung, Roberto Assagioli, Frederick Perls, and Eric Berne. Their ideas form the basis for some of the concepts presented in the book.

Few, however, will know the tremendous help I received from many others. Michael Rosenbaum, M.D., an orthomolecular psychiatrist on the staff of the Wholistic Health and Nutrition Institute in Mill Valley, California, was immeasurably helpful in checking the appendix for accuracy. Winifred Van Etten and Carolyn Hardesty, both writers, offered much encouragement on the beginning stages of the manuscript. Dorothy Stewart, Ph.D., a counseling psychologist, gave excellent suggestions about some of the underlying concepts in Part I. Throughout the project, Richard Peterson, Ph.D., an organizational sociologist, was involved in looking over two complete drafts. Not only do I respect his keen insight, but I also value his strong support, which he gave so freely along the way. Toward the end, Mary Ellen Carew arrived on the scene, like a fairy godmother. A writer, an artist, an editor, and a wonderful friend, she put refining touches on the manuscript. Then, Carol Brokel took the project in tow, typing with characteristic speed and deciphering roadmap-like directions with patience and marvelous good humor. Finally, Alan Moores gave expert advice on tightening the text.

To this wonderful group of friends, I am indeed grateful. They helped to form what I like to consider a philosophical primer for performers.

PART ONE

The Process

CHAPTER 1

Stagefright and the Performer

PERFORMERS KNOW THE MOMENT of magic when it comes. It comes to the actor, whether on Broadway or in a neighborhood playhouse; to the musician, whether on the international circuit or the local scene; to the athlete, whether in Yankee Stadium or on a sandlot diamond. Business professionals, teachers, lawyers, club leaders capture the moment as well. And all who do, share a similar delight, whether for an instant, an hour, or an evening. Something about their performance "clicks into gear," and they feel on top of the task, swept away by the occasion. There is a rush of satisfaction, even a point of exaltation when all their powers converge on the matter at hand. They become so immersed, so caught up in the action that they feel "connected" with the performance, in some way expanded by the event. This feeling of expansion and connection is the moment of magic. For those who have experienced it, there is nothing that compares.

Those of us who know about these moments of magic look

forward to an approaching performance (especially when it exists in the comfortable, distant future). We anticipate an exciting game, an important business deal, or a special speech or concert, dreaming of how we hope the event will go. For weeks ahead we rehearse before the mirror or silently in our heads, enjoying that special moment in fantasy.

Somewhere along the line, however, as the date draws closer, the fantasy begins to dim, our enthusiasm dwindles, and that unmistakable feeling we have known before wells up. Hands turn clammy, knees begin to shake, and a myriad of thoughts swirl in our heads.

- "The team is depending on me. What if I let them down?"
- "If I lose *this* deal, I'll be out a job."
- "What if I forget in the middle? I'll just *die* on the spot."

In short, we have bumped up against that peculiar bane of all performers—stagefright. Stagefright has eclipsed the coming performance, and we seem blocked from the pleasure and excitement we have long anticipated.

What is the nature of this block and how does it stand in the way of our pleasure? How does it impede our abilities and our functioning? Most important, how can we move *through* the block so that its nervous tension can be turned into productive energy for performance? These are the central questions we will want to answer in this book.

SPECIFICS OF STAGEFRIGHT

The fear of losing face while under the eye of public scrutiny is the foundation of stagefright. If we fail privately, we seem less concerned, because we can keep it more or less a secret from the world at large. Stagefright, on the other hand, carries with it the dread of possible public failure and the consequent shame of public humiliation.

Stimulating this dread is a strong sense of anticipation, which reaches an agitated peak immediately before the big event, even though it may have been in the making for days. The quivers may or may not continue during the performance, but generally they calm fairly quickly afterward—certainly by the next day. Thus stagefright, when compared to other forms of anxiety, occurs within a relatively short time.

This rather short time period contributes to the enormous pressure that performers feel, but this is only one of several pressure factors associated with stagefright. Training and preparation are exceedingly rigorous. Many performers spend untold hours, years even, preparing for an event in which a split second could spell disaster. Mistakes are costly. Either the goal is made, the right note played, or it is missed, and we cannot interrupt the play and ask, "Let me try it again."

Besides the threat of mistakes, the expectations one senses from others also exert heavy pressure. We feel we must live up to the demands of coaches, teachers, parents, or the audience. And blanketing the entire pressure picture is the whole issue of winning or losing. If we win, we are good; if we lose, we are bad, as if decreed by law.

These factors—the preparation, the desire to win or to meet expectations, the costly mistakes, and the short time span—not only create the pressure felt by performers, but they also explain the existence of countless performers who, though eminently talented and thoroughly trained, have serious difficulties in performing at the high level of which they are capable.

Stagefright and Role Adoptions

The work of the actor, athlete, musician, and the like does not provide society with the basic material necessities of life, as does that of, say, the farmer, doctor, or house builder. Although the pursuits of performers contribute immeasurably to the quality of life, their tasks carry a certain hint of illusion, one step removed from everyday existence. Adding to this quality of illusion is the fact that many performers use the body and the voice in a stylized way. The body, while usually quite functional at walking, eating, and other daily routines, requires rigorous training to perfect the movements of ballet, football, or playing a musical instrument. Singers and actors likewise practice to use the voice in a stylized way, different from ordinary speech. Consequently, a performer is sharply aware of functioning in a very specialized way. For this reason, however, many performers develop definite, preconceived ideas about how persons in their particular field *should* perform; therefore, they perform in a stereotyped way. They adopt a role that they feel fits a certain image, or persona.

Each profession has its persona. To get an idea of the persona associated with a particular group, imagine attending a convention of athletes, and then one for musicians. Certainly we would see a contrast, but we could make even finer distinctions. At an athletic convention most of us could distinguish the football players from the tennis players, and few would confuse rock musicians with opera stars.

By adopting certain roles, however, many performers double-perform. They function not only as performers, but they also follow the stereotyped *role* of a performer, as if to play out a script.

A famous opera singer tells the story that she auditioned eight times for a leading opera company and was not accepted. On the ninth time, however, she literally let her hair down, wore an off-the-shoulder red dress rather than the usual formal black one, and won a part. It is doubtful that her singing had improved so dramatically this final time around but obvious that she had dropped her stereotyped role as the opera singer.

ROLES AND VULNERABILITY

Stereotyped roles are adopted, mostly unwittingly, as a defense against stagefright. They seemingly preserve our public image and thus protect our private self from vulnerability.

Nature, however, has instilled in us a primitive reaction to vulnerability. Early cave dwellers, upon meeting danger to their existence, say a tiger, responded immediately, by either fighting or fleeing. Using instinct, which produces very specific and dramatic changes in the body, they protected themselves from extinction.

Stagefright, on the other hand, is an imagined fear that usually presents no physical danger to our lives. The fear that a public appearance threatens our life is imagined (although this fear can reduce our bodies to a paralyzed mass). What is actually threatened is our sense of identity, our self-esteem and pride, rather than actual life and breath. Nevertheless it *feels* fatal and our protection response is stimulated. Because we are docile, "cultivated" persons of the twentieth century, however, we do not flee or fight. We do nothing, realizing that the enemy is only imaginary and that "nice" people remain composed. Thus, in an effort to remain calm, but at the same time at least pay lip-service to our protective instinct, we adopt a specific role identification.

Unfortunately, such restrictive identifications are precisely the ones that produce the feelings of vulnerability we hope to avoid. If, however, we identify ourselves with much broader archetypal concepts—such as being a man or woman, a learner, or a child of the universe—the daily fluctuations of adversity pale to insignificance. We do not feel vulnerable because we are a man, woman, or even an American. We feel so because we identify ourselves with a more specific idea which for one reason or other is important to us: "I am the main after-dinner speaker for the President's Club," "I am the twelfth-grade English teacher at Riverdale High," or, "I am the coach for the National Cyclones." Such narrow role identifications distort our self-concept, since as human beings we embody much more than they imply. Moreover, in maintaining such a narrow sense of identity, our self-concept is tested with each performance, and the more important the occasion, the more likely this identification faces possible devastation. If a performance fails to meet expectations, we begin to assume that "I am unworthy." Not only that, specific role identifications make us feel isolated —"me against them"—and, consequently, more vulnerable.

It is true, of course, that idiosyncratic roles may be necessary on some level to provide the performer an appropriate vehicle to carry out specific functions. Being the football coach for the National Cyclones or the prima ballerina of the Royal Theatre carries some definite requirements that help us to focus clearly on what we want to convey.

Without our being acutely aware of our roles, however, and the extent to which we "play" them, extremely narrow role identifications can turn into "antiscripts," roles that funnel us into the exact opposite direction. Even if a performer is riding the crest of success, new fears of failure may crop up with each new achievement. We may be an audience favorite, but as our star rises higher and higher the more frightened we become. We become "dual scripted."

Let's say the National Cyclones coach has had a winning streak. He may unconsciously begin to play the "National Cyclones coach who needs to win." The more he feels he must win, the more afraid he becomes of losing. He then becomes the pessimistic victor, for whom each new win brings an additional threat.

Naturally, such roles are riddled with self-deception. Moreover, they represent only a small part of our true nature. But most important for us, adopting specific and stereotyped roles creates more stagefright. Perhaps an example I hold in vivid memory will illustrate more specifically how this happens.

The self-protection role I scripted for myself with unflagging vigor I now call in retrospect the Master Teacher. This script was specifically connected to my career as a college professor and was created to help me combat the stagefright I associated with lecturing in class. Its major premise was absolutely never let a student find out how dumb you really are, or you'll turn to dust.

The first day I met a college class, there I was, twenty-three years old, a certified adult, fresh out of graduate school, and without a shred of experience in making a class presentation. I had spent weeks preparing for this fifty-minute session. Had I been a statesman, I would have had enough lecture material to present a week-long conference at the U.N.! Nevertheless, on that first day of class the inner voice directing my script broadcast on a clear channel: "Careful now. Those students are going to be on the lookout. You don't want them to see how green you are. Stay calm. Better yet, scare the hell out of 'em and they'll never notice how scared you are."

I plunged in. "Good morning. I am Robert Triplett." My greeting was calm and calculated, marred only by the fact that I could not as yet place in front of my name that universal certification of brilliance—"Doctor." ("Uh oh," said the voice.)

"First, let me establish the peripheries of the course, giving you the goals and expectations I have of each member of the class. We have a lot, er, much ("Watch it!") material to cover. Outside preparation will require a minimum of two hours for each hour of class. ("Good," went the voice, "look at 'em squirm at *that*.") Furthermore, the standards of excellence will be high." And on and on.

Thus I felt my vulnerability was protected. From whom? The students. They of course became the enemy who might discover my weakness. (We do not need protection from friends!) This hard-nosed attitude at a superficial level did have certain benefits. Everyone worked hard, we learned a lot, and the students respected my teaching. But we were terrified of each other. (It occurs to me now how much "educating" goes on in an atmosphere of fear.) There was another catch, too. Any confidence I gained from the students' respect seemed counterfeit. I perceived they respected not so much me, but the role I presented. Therefore any compliment I received rang hollow, since I attributed it to the facade. True, whenever a student offered a good word about a lecture I always responded with a gracious thank you, but inwardly I was saying, "Oh boy, if they only knew how hard I worked on this lecture, they might not think I'm so smart," or worse yet, "Wonder why they're being so nice today?" The script ruled out my hearing compliments because that would invalidate the script's raison d'être. So I discounted any kind word. Consequently, every year the first lectures brought on more stagefright. The experience I was accumulating seemed not to suffice. For me the antidote for stagefright was not experience or thorough preparation, as I had been led to believe. Where, then, did it lie? I decided to see.

On one particular occasion, when for some reason my class preparation had gone poorly, I decided to chance an experiment. Rather than trying to cover my lack of preparation with steel-like defensiveness, I admitted my predicament. "I'm sorry. Today I don't feel very well prepared. I'll need your help." Quite honestly the words were a shock to me as well as to them, but we all rallied and a lively discussion carried us through the day. It was an exciting class for all, but especially for me. I learned a lot. I did not need to give up class preparation, but I also did not need to feign being a scholastic dictator. I found that when I loosened the reins, the students assumed much more class responsibility. Most of all I learned a simple lasting lesson—since admitting vulnerability was no longer a threat, I did not need protection from it. Out of my "weakness" had come a stimulating session. The weakness had been my perception, my reality.

In retrospect, how simple it all seems to greet others with trust, for when we give up our compulsion for protection, our feelings of vulnerability vanish with the role we discard.

Unfortunately, scripted behavior eludes simplicity, because maintaining a script seems to carry less risk—on the surface. Scripts are a product of habit and are therefore predictable, thus giving the illusion of safety. In actuality, they lock us into the very predicament they were formulated to avoid. I adopted the Master Teacher script to project a protective persona.

As my persona grew, however, so did my stagefright and vulnerability.

Vulnerability and protectionism perpetuate each other. If we continue to protect ourselves, we heighten our self-*consciousness*, but not our self-*awareness*. As our self-consciousness grows, so does our need for protection because we have become a bigger target. With bigger targets comes stronger defense, and so the two swell together.

Stagefright, vulnerability, self-protection, and self-assurance form an involved configuration. It seems logical on one level that if we experience stagefright and feel vulnerable, we must follow our instincts to protect ourselves. If we succeed, confidence should be ours; but such confidence rests on a very precarious level. We may show confidence on the outside but lack inner security because of the vicious circle we set up between vulnerability and protection. We never reach honest assurance.

Real assurance is found in a seemingly strange way. It is found by our giving up our protective measures and willfully entering into the block of stagefright. As odd as this may seem, if we enter this realm and accept whatever we may find, we will begin to move *through* the block of stagefright toward new qualities on the other side. In this process, stagefright is converted into a totally new phenomenon. As we shall see, it becomes a quality that proves valuable for our performance.

Our first job, however, is to look into the block, because that is where the journey begins. The block of stagefright contains the impetus that leads us to the other side.

CHAPTER 2

Entering
into Stagefright

IN THE WORKSHOPS ON STAGEFRIGHT that I have led across the country, no two persons have ever entered the stagefright block in precisely the same way. Moreover, no two have found exactly the same qualities on the other side. Thus the experience is a unique affair. But all who have entered the block without preconceptions have shared in a common experience. They have been significantly enlightened by what they discovered.

In one such workshop Frank,* a lawyer, reported that whenever he spoke in court, he held a constant fear that his voice would quaver and that others might see his hands shaking. In essence, he was afraid of losing control. I asked him to read an abstract for the group and, while doing so, to consciously shake the paper as he read. He read very well, with an easy, modulated voice, even though the paper was indeed shaking wildly.

---

*To preserve confidentiality, names and certain professional data in this and other accounts have been changed. The essential content, however, remains intact.

Eventually he stopped in amazement and declared, "I'm having trouble getting the paper to shake!"

With a flash of insight, he arrived at a discovery: in choosing to shake, he had entered the block so long avoided and, in doing so, dissipated its energy. By selecting noncontrol, rather than letting it choose him, he placed himself in the driver's seat, so to speak, and gained control of events over which he previously had no power. In this particular instance, the energy in the block was released fairly quickly because Frank was willing to suspend his expectations and see what the block might have to offer. Sometimes, however, our misconceptions about what qualities we need in performance make it difficult for us to discern what exactly is in the block and what is not. Beth's experience is typical.

When asked what she would like to be able to do when she performed, Beth, a guitarist, replied that she wanted to concentrate on the music and control her performance. (Such a response is typical of highly trained performers, musicians or not.) I asked her what got in the way of her concentration and her control, and she said, "Well, I feel tense and 'spastic.' "

I then asked if she would be willing to enter into the block, to be deliberately tense and "spastic" in order to see what energies might be there that could help her through this obstruction.

"You mean play tense and spastic right now? I'm not sure. It goes against everything I've been taught."

"I know," I replied. "It's like desecrating yourself and the music, yet there may be some quality in being tense and spastic that might be useful to you in finding the control and concentration you seek."

With some reluctance she agreed to experiment a bit just to see what would happen.

I instructed her first to let her body become as tense as possible and then begin to play.

Drawing herself into such a hard knot she scarcely could move, Beth had to strain just to get her fingers to pluck the strings. It wasn't easy. Every note was difficult and forced. When she could play no more, I asked, "Now, how would you be if you were spastic? Exaggerate those feelings and when they penetrate your whole body, begin to play."

With trembling hands and quaking shoulders, Beth took up the guitar again and jerkily stuttered through each note.

"Now return to the tension," I directed.

This time her arms were not held with such drastic contraction; they moved with the slightest gesture.

"Go back to being spastic," I said.

This switch revealed some slight changes, also. Beth's spastic movements were a bit larger and less jerky than at first. She continued swinging back and forth between the opposite stances. As she did, her tense position acquired more movement and her spastic motions grew larger and less cramped. Finally, after about eight rounds of this, the opposing positions were hardly distinguishable. Beth's movements, although a little excessive, were nevertheless comfortable and were graceful to watch.

"What did you discover?" I asked.

"Well, when I was tense, I found out that's how I usually control my playing and concentrate on the music; but when I was spastic, it occurred to me that I wanted to move and not be so rigid."

Beth discovered that control, contrary to what she had thought from behind the block of stagefright, was not what she needed after all. In fact, she was overcontrolled, so much so that she had had no freedom when performing. The spastic movements, she learned, grew out of a longing for liberty never allowed. Since any free movements had been rigidly harnessed, they (not to be denied some expression) had changed into tremulous jerks, which she had tried to control. However, the more she tried to control them, the jerkier they became. On allowing the jerks to come to the surface, though, and seeing them in contrast to gripping immobility, she saw that control—or actually overcontrol—was indeed part of the block and that the quality she actually sought was one of freedom. But she discovered this only by entering the block.

VALIDATING THE SYMPTOMS

The accounts of Frank and Beth demonstrate symptoms that plague practically every performer, and in almost every case they are brought about by an attempt to stifle those symptoms, rather than to accept them. With the first tremor of stagefright we think to ourselves, "I can't shake now; I must control myself." But the control we seek is a mutated variety linked to tension. We become tense to avoid making mistakes, especially if our task entails delicate maneuvers. But tension impedes movement, and holding still stimulates the need to move. If the natural movement is thwarted, it erupts into spasmodic shakes. In both accounts related above, the performers began to move through the stagefright block only after *validating* the symptoms they previously tried to avoid.

MENTAL IMAGERY

Many performers find it helpful to validate their symptoms through the use of mental imagery. Whenever I have asked performers to "see" what stagefright looks like in their imagination, I am always amazed at the rich variety of images that come up: a weight on the shoulders, a whirlwind, a green Martian, Mother, a fortress, a tank, a pointing finger, Daddy, Jell-O, a wavy yellow line—the list could go on. Images do not have to be visual either. They can and do involve any of the five senses and perhaps a mood, emotion, or inner sensation. Being tense and spastic presents a graphic mental image, although not necessarily visual. Still, many are unaware of their images, even though they may hold a storehouseful. This was true of Joe.

Joe knew very well the physical symptoms of stagefright. He experienced bodily shaking for about the first five minutes each time he began to perform; he was afraid he might fall or drop his instrument, which he clutched tightly to avoid losing it.

On being asked to fantasize an image to help him describe his feelings, Joe reported he had no image, no thoughts, and no ideas about what might be the matter. He just felt "bad" and didn't know why.

"How do you mean, 'bad'?" I asked.

"I don't know. It's sort of a flitting, illusive feeling—as though for a split second I might suddenly be paralyzed."

"Describe that flitting feeling and tell me what it is like."

"I'm not sure. It's almost like a bat that sweeps down so fast I can't even see it."

"Give the bat a voice and see what it has to say to you."

"It simply zips by with these warnings, 'Look out for that high note, you're gonna split it. You'll pinch the tone if you're not careful.' "

I asked Joe if he had any response to the bat.

"Yes. 'Go away and leave me alone. You mess everything up.' "

I then suggested, "Let's imagine the bat can play your instrument. Describe how it would play."

"Dreadful. Notes would be split and the tone would be squawky. Just the way he's telling *me* not to play."

I asked Joe if he would be willing to demonstrate the bat's playing, just to see what it would feel like. On trying this experiment, Joe played with a somewhat piercing tone, but very accurately. I asked him to check back with the bat for any reactions.

"Well, the bat has changed. He's now a huge, scary animal."

"What does he say to you?"

"Nothing. He won't say anything. He just gets bigger and bigger."

"For a few minutes imagine that you are the scary animal. Actually become the animal, and assume a body posture that suggests his actions."

Joe reared up in his chair and puffed his chest out in a display of brute strength. I spoke to the "animal."

"What is it that you're not going to tell Joe?"

"I'm not going to tell him the truth because Joe is scared of it." The voice was deep; although gruff, it showed resonance.

"And what is the truth that Joe is afraid of?"

"He's afraid he will find out he's not as good as he ought to be."

"And how good is that?"

"Perfect. If he doesn't play perfectly, he's no good."

I then asked Joe if this were true. Confronted with this possibility, he said he would be unhappy if he believed he had not met his own standards, yet deep down he knew how he played did not affect his total worth as a person.

At this point, the image changed again—this time into a half-man, half-animal. The creature told Joe he was afraid of being vulnerable. Upon reflection, Joe realized that to escape feeling vulnerable, he had overcontrolled his performance to avoid mistakes.

"And what are you doing right now, Joe, being vulnerable or controlled?" I asked.

"Very vulnerable, but I'm being honest."

"And how does that feel—to be honest?"

"I'm much more relaxed now than earlier. It seems the more vulnerable I become, the more honest I feel. Yet as I grow more honest, the feelings of vulnerability subside and I am able to relax; the tension seems to release. I'm beginning to see that my stagefright comes from something I'm doing to myself. It doesn't come from other people's judgments, but from my own self-criticism."

Joe began to see that his stagefright came from a part of himself that felt insecure and vulnerable. Yet he understood that the more he accepted vulnerability, the more secure he became. With this revelation the image once more changed, this time into a magician who told Joe that his talent had an element of magic in it and that he needed to let go of his rigid control in order to allow the music's mystery to unfold. He needed to trust his inner magic.

The transformation of images in Joe's experience is similar to that of many who explore stagefright through visualization. In many cases those images gradually assume more human forms, and with each new image, the message takes a different turn. At first it may be elusive, then threatening, later consoling, until finally it becomes a source of insight.

As Joe chose to move through the stagefright block, certain elements from the other side of the block flickered into play. The first was his realization that the way he played did not reflect his total worth as a person. Next, he began to see the relationship between honesty and vulnerability in performance and that worth is revealed in both. Finally, he heard the compelling words of the magician, who spoke of the richness of his talent and its element of magic.

Enrichment in one form or another is what came to light in all three of these accounts. Although Frank, Beth, and Joe each approached their particular problems in an individual way, all entered into stagefright and saw it change into a quality that was valuable to their performance. A major factor in their success was their acceptance of the block—the fact that they were willing to receive whatever emerged in the encounter.

Accepting the block, however, is not always easy, because stagefright produces in us a jumble of thoughts and feelings. Our journey to the other side will be made easier if we have an idea of what thoughts and feelings *might* surface along the way.

CHAPTER 3

Stagefright
and Thoughts

THOUGHTS AND FEELINGS, of course, are integrally related. Thoughts influence our moods and shape our actions. Any thoughts we have about performance are eventually revealed in whatever performance we undertake. But the reverse is equally true. Our moods shape our thoughts, and this is what we want to look at now: the influence of stagefright on the way we think.

To aid in our discussion, I have adapted a model of the human personality introduced by Roberto Assagioli. Assagioli, the creator of a school of philosophy called "psychosynthesis," sees three levels in our inner makeup (figure 3.1).

The Lower Unconscious contains prime instincts, directed mainly at self-preservation, that can be stimulated by stagefright if they remain outside our awareness. With conscious recognition, however, their energy can be transformed into productive aids for performance.

Opposite the lower level is the Higher Unconscious, which

19

Figure 3.1. The Psychosynthesis Model

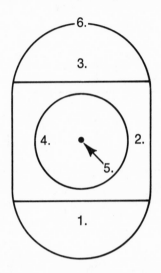

1. The Lower Unconscious
2. The Middle Unconscious
3. The Higher Unconscious or Superconscious
4. The Field of Consciousness
5. The Conscious Self or "I"
   (The Observing "I")
6. The Higher Self

Source: Roberto Assagioli, M.D., *Psychosynthesis* (Hobbs, Dorman & Co., Inc., 1965). Reprinted by permission of The Sterling Lord Agency, Inc. Copyright © 1965 by Psychosynthesis Research Foundation.

Author's note: The Observing "I," noted in parentheses, is my addition. That is the term used in some circles in the field of psycho-synthesis and is the one we will use throughout the book. Also, in the original, there is a seventh item that lies outside the diagram which represents the Collective Unconscious. I have omitted this item, because the concept of the collective unconscious is beyond the scope of this book.

contains the Higher Self. Here are born ideas, insights, intuitions, and hunches. What interests us now is the middle level, the mediator between the two. In order for the energies of the lower level to be transformed and those of the upper level to be manifested, they must be brought into the middle area of conscious awareness. This is where thoughts take place.

Conscious Awareness

In thinking about our personality, we realize that we as human beings embrace a dichotomy. On the one hand, we are multidimensional, behaving differently in varying circumstances. For example, we act one way at a football game and another way in an art gallery—almost like different persons. Sometimes we are happy; other times, sad. We could fill a page with different characteristics, perceptions, and habits. On the other hand, something about us stays the same. The same "I" who went to bed last night arises the next morning. Who we are constitutes both endless variety and, at the same time, steadfast continuity. This continuous identity is called the Observing "I." It is the center of the personality around which revolve the diverse qualities just mentioned, called "subpersonalities"—numerous semi-autonomous manifestations of the Observing "I."

Subpersonalities create the voices inside our heads and influence us to make identifications that change with circumstances. Whenever we become unwittingly identified with a subpersonality, objective observation becomes distorted. We are pulled off-center, so to speak, and look at the world from a reduced perspective.

To allow an objective observation of these subpersonalities and to facilitate an understanding of them, many persons give their subpersonalities descriptive names. (Labeling the voices in our heads is a practice found in several counseling traditions —transactional analysis, psychosynthesis, and gestalt therapy, to name three.) Thus, the Perfectionist might denote a subpersonality that strives for an errorless performance, the Doubter, one that questions our performing abilities.

Subpersonalities chatter freely in our heads, commenting on practically everything that happens to us in our waking moments. Often, however, conversation takes place between those that are dually opposed. For example, an Organizer which says, "You've got an important board meeting tomorrow, you'd better get those facts firmly fixed in your head," may stimulate a Free Spirit which counters with, "But it's such a nice day; what fun it would be to hike in the woods."

DUAL OPPOSITES

The dual-opposite connection between subpersonalities is a fascinating principle, and one directly related to our understanding of stagefright. The conceptual part of the mind—that which is traditionally considered the rational, intellectual segment of our faculties—accumulates knowledge by experiencing dual opposites. It grasps the meaning of a particular concept by contrasting that concept with its antithesis. The intellect conceptualizes the quality of "hot" by knowing also the quality of "cold." It understands smoothness within the context of roughness and strength within the experience of weakness. Conceptual reality depends upon the knowledge of dual opposites. That is how we make sense of the world.

Another dimension also rises from the concept of dual opposites—that of integration. If we know both "hot" and "cold," we can conceptualize their integration, the quality of "warm." Yet, without knowing the interaction between the dual, or polar, opposites, we cannot grasp the integrated quality. For instance, if we lived our entire lives in a seventy-degree climate, we could not know "warm" because we would not have felt "cold" or "hot," even though both are found in "warm." In fact, "warm" would cease to be a perceived reality because we would have no standard of comparison. In this simple illustration we find three dynamics at work: "hot," "cold," and the integration of the two, the quality of "warm." The last, however, can be comprehended only within the parameters of the other two.

Conscious awareness grows from the experience of dual opposites—the one against the other—and their subsequent integration. Two other elementary examples of this polar integration can be selected: abstinence versus indulgence yields temperance; hardness versus softness yields suppleness.

Polar opposites, however—and this is the problem—are not so easily recognizable in more complicated circumstances—those associated more directly with performance, for example. This is especially true with regard to subpersonalities. A dichotomy may be missed when one subpersonality is highly vocal and the other is not, and we leave unnoticed the subpersonality that is silenced by the first. For example, a subpersonality that wants to control every situation activates in some way an opposite subpersonality that longs to give freedom, but this part of the dichotomy may be overlooked. Likewise, a doubting subpersonality awakens another that wants to offer conviction; a subpersonality that confuses every issue activates one that can clarify. In each of these cases we may miss the polarity if we become identified with the active subpersonality, and neglect the one that is passive.

When their polar opposites are neglected, subpersonalities give up their search for their inverted twins and begin to cluster around particular issues, finding kin in their own camp, so to speak. This happens with stagefright; they cluster around the issue, becoming so embroiled that they completely overlook the dual opposites with which they initially hoped to establish contact.

THE STAGEFRIGHT CLUSTER

We can see how a typical cluster of stagefright subpersonalities might be drawn together if we reflect a moment on our performance. All of us hold certain ideal concepts of what an impending performance ought to be—standards set by ourselves or others. As the performance draws nigh, however, we begin to doubt our ability to meet these standards, and with that doubt we become irritated with ourselves that we might not measure up. The doubt and self-condemnation combine, moreover, to kindle the fear that we will be totally incapable of satisfying *any* standards whatsoever. Our thought patterns in stagefright center on these three issues: doubt, criticism, and fear. Thus these are the issues around which develops the cluster of stagefright subpersonalities.

Following our earlier lead to label subpersonalities, we can call the subpersonality associated with criticism, the Critic; the one with doubt, the Doubter; and the one with fear, the Weakling (for reasons soon obvious).

THE POLAR INTERPLAY

Remembering the polarity principle, we can see that each of the subpersonalities searches for a dual opposite. The Doubter seeks a subpersonality with an answer to the problem. The Critic, having a condemning nature, looks for a subpersonality that can offer commendation. And the Weakling longs for a subpersonality of strength.

Put another way, all the qualities of stagefright—doubt, criticism, and fear—are polar opposites of qualities we value in performance. Rather than doubt our abilities, we would like to believe in ourselves, to have self-assurance and conviction. In addition, we hope to give a commendable performance, not one that will create adverse criticism. And last, rather than feeling frightened, we would prefer to have courage. We can sum up the polar relation between the qualities of stagefright and those we value this way:

doubt opposes belief
criticism opposes commendation
fear opposes courage

Moreover, just as we named the subpersonalities associated with stagefright, we can do the same with the qualities we value. The subpersonality that expresses assurance, or belief in ourselves, we can call the Believer; the one that manifests commendation, the Commender; and the one that demonstrates courage, we can designate the Risker.

In lining up the stagefright subpersonalities opposite the ones that represent their valued, polar qualities (figure 3.2) we can see a subtle relationship between the two sides.

Figure 3.2. Subpersonality Polarities

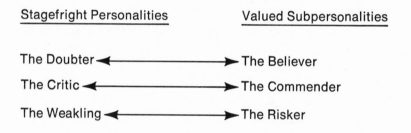

Stagefright Personalities   Valued Subpersonalities

The Doubter ⟵⟶ The Believer

The Critic ⟵⟶ The Commender

The Weakling ⟵⟶ The Risker

Although the two groups show contradiction, each valued subpersonality depends on its polar opposite for manifestation. The Believer cannot exist without the Doubter, since belief comes as a result of having doubted. Had we never doubted our abilities, we could never have made any discoveries about our competency; and with each discovery, belief in our abilities increases. Consequently, through doubt, belief grows stronger.

This same interrelation applies to the other polar constructs. Criticism and commendation depend on each other for verification. To develop good judgment, we must observe proficiencies as well as deficiencies. Furthermore, commendation without criticism (or vice versa) loses a point of comparison, and as a result, becomes worthless. Similarly, fear and courage fit together, also, in that courage involves a willingness to risk danger. Were there no danger, there would be no need for courage. One acknowledges the other.

Stagefright, then, has a vital function in our obtaining the qualities we hope to achieve. But the question arises: Why are these qualities unavailable before a performance?

THE PERFORMER'S POSITION

At the outset, we suggested that stagefright blocks the performer from the excitement of a coming performance. We can picture a diagram of this situation showing the performer behind the block of stagefright with his or her view of the coming performance cut off (figure 3.3).

Figure 3.3 The Approaching Performance

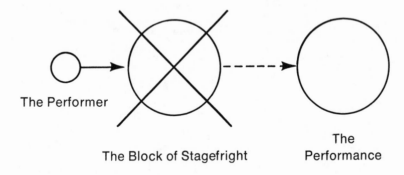

The Performer

The Block of Stagefright

The Performance

Now, if we superimpose this diagram onto the psychosynthesis model, we get a concept slightly different. We can call this combined figure the Performer's Matrix, since it suggests an archetype, or universal pattern, that influences nearly every performer (figure 3.4).

The performer's matrix shows that the performer has been pulled off-center from the Observing "I" position to that of an

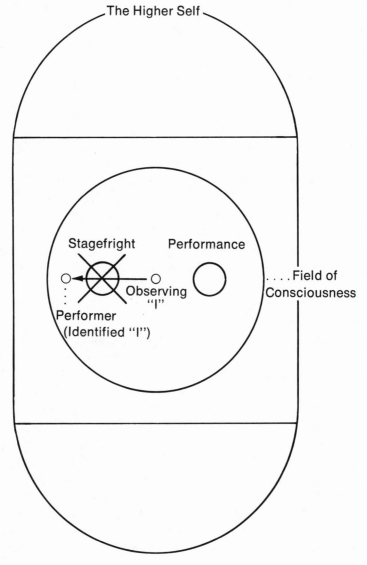

Figure 3.4. The Performer's Matrix

Identified "I." In this identified position the performer cannot see the larger picture and therefore perceives the issues of doubt, criticism, and fear as independent entities, isolated from the larger purpose. This means, of course, that the subpersonalities linked with these issues are cut off from their polar opposites. As a result, they begin to mutate their energy, changing into something more insidious.

The Doubter becomes increasingly doubtful, almost a relentless inquisitor, questioning our every move. With the questions coming ever faster, the energy of doubt turns to alarm and reaches, in its advanced level, a state of confusion. Similarly, the attitude of the Critic turns to contempt, like that of a cynic; what may have begun as minor irritation expands to outright anger. Following the same line, the Weakling grows weaker still and assumes the status of an impotent victim whose fear turns into panic.

This condition—the confused Doubter, the angry Critic, and the panic-stricken Weakling—describes the stagefright cluster as it operates without the balancing qualities from the other side. It is a mutated condition.

MUTATED OPPOSITES

Even mutated states seek polar opposites, however. That is to say, a mutated quality seeks an equally mutated opponent. When stagefright subpersonalities operate without the benefit of their natural counterparts, they turn to aberrant opposites. The Inquisitor-Doubter demands fixed and irrefutable answers from a Dogmatist subpersonality; the Cynic-Critic craves an absolute (though unobtainable) exactness as espoused by a Perfectionist; and the Victim-Weakling searches for an iron-clad defense, as promised by a Protector.

The notion begins to stir—"If only I had absolute certainty" (like the Dogmatist), "If only I could be guaranteed a flawless performance" (as fancied by the Perfectionist), "If only I had absolutely nothing to fear" (as claimed by the Protector). But these are the qualities of the *mutated* opposites, and they are caricatures of the natural polarities. They emanate from the Identified "I" position, from what it *thinks* to be the answer to its troubles because the block of stagefright prevents it from seeing the natural opposites.

To get a clearer picture of the situation, we can think of these qualities as having been projected by the Identified "I" to a place just below the natural opposites (figure 3.5).

Figure 3.5.   The Performer's Matrix with Mutated Opposites

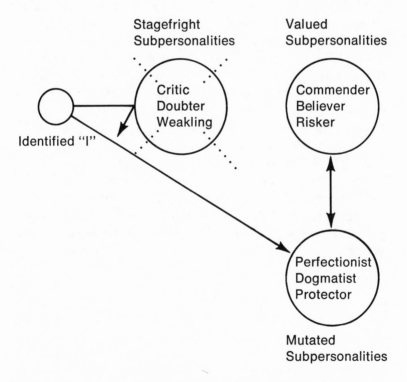

Stagefright
Subpersonalities

Valued
Subpersonalities

Critic
Doubter
Weakling

Commender
Believer
Risker

Identified "I"

Perfectionist
Dogmatist
Protector

Mutated
Subpersonalities

In effect, with a new line of sight established, the Observing "I" assumes that by moving along this line, it can avoid the block of stagefright. Even though the assumption is false, it is the basis for the way in which most of us deal with stagefright. Thus, when messages of self-doubt, criticism, and fear begin to grind in our heads, we try to snuff them out and substitute something else in their place. We think along these lines:

"Uh, oh. You're doubting yourself. You're getting confused and scared! Gads! You can't afford to doubt now. You've got to look confident. You can't be confused. You must control yourself and be strong."

Far from providing any relief, such a response actually draws us unwittingly into the whirlwind we hope to avoid.

The Dogmatist tells the Doubter he* must stop doubting. "Think positively," he says. But the Doubter wonders how he can think positively when the last performance was next to failure. The Perfectionist prescribes control to avoid mistakes, but the Critic wonders how control is possible when frustration reaches the boiling point. Similarly, the Protector orders brute confidence, yet the Weakling is shaking like a leaf. None of the stagefright subpersonalities trust their mutated opposites, but at the same time, the more they tangle, the more they tantalize. This is how we get lured into stagefright.

The mutated subpersonalities give a solution to stagefright that sounds correct. The remedy they propose seems to be logical. But in reality these little "dictators" *are* the problem. They pull us in deeper, because the answers they give are usually wrong.

---

*Subpersonalities are, of course, genderless, but for the sake of readability, I will use the masculine pronoun when referring to them.

CHAPTER 4

Pinpointing
the Stagefright Voices

FINDING THE RIGHT ANSWERS depends in part on our knowing where the *wrong* answers are coming from. If we are able to pinpoint the stagefright voices, we can better evaluate what we hear. Thus, we want to look closely at the stagefright subpersonalities and their mutated opposites to see what qualities they possess, what messages they send out, and what part they play in the internal drama. This will allow a more objective appraisal of the voices that buzz in our heads.

Although the mutated subpersonalities are projected outside the cluster, in actuality they are part of the block, since they emanate from the cluster itself. They represent the desires of the stagefright group. The Critic desires an absolute standard as represented by the Perfectionist, the Doubter seeks the guarantee of success promised by the Dogmatist, and the Weakling craves the Protector's defensive shield. Thus, in effect, the cluster contains six subpersonalities, and we shall list here in polar pairs, although transactions can occur from any one to the other:

Critic/Perfectionist
Doubter/Dogmatist
Weakling/Protector

Which subpersonality speaks first is not always easy to make
out, but most performers probably hear the Doubter first, since
his voice is activated early in the game.

DOUBTER/DOGMATIST

The mark of the Doubter is uncertainty and his messages can
begin well in advance of a particular event, when we hear in our
heads all manner of questions and announcements concerning
the approaching date. Responding to the calendar, his is the
voice that ticks off the days beforehand:

"Only three more weeks 'til opening night. Think you'll be
ready? You need at least six more weeks to memorize the lines,
and there's that difficult scene in Act III."

The Doubter is future-oriented, constantly wondering about
the possible outcome. His favorite question begins with "what
if"—What if I drop the ball? What if I fluff a line? What if I
draw a blank? And so forth. Sometimes his questions and announcements are accompanied by a mental image of someone
with thin, tight lips looking over our shoulder. Each mistake is
met with raised eyebrows and a nodding head that affirms, "See,
I told you so. Better be careful."

In reality, the Doubter is searching for reinforcement from
the Believer outside the cluster, but none is forthcoming because of the cut-off position of the Identified "I." More likely,
his comments stimulate the Weakling, who responds, "Oh gee,
you're right. I'll probably botch the whole thing." This unsatis-
factory response causes the Doubter's energy to mutate, where-
upon he turns from prudent inquirer to skeptical inquisitor. In
this mutated condition, he seeks an answer from his mutated
opposite, the Dogmatist. The Dogmatist, activated by doubt,
supplies fail-proof answers for the Doubter: "You're not think-

ing clearly. What you need is concentration on the business at hand." Or, "You're thinking negatively. You've got to think positively."

Although the responses seem logical, they offer little assurance, since they give no credence to the Doubter's present condition. The Doubter is told to stop being what he is. His integrity is rebuffed. This causes him to move closer to the Weakling, who laments to the Dogmatist, "Gosh, I can't concentrate now. Help!"

At this point the Critic, feeling increasingly frustrated, might enter the scene: "You're going to screw up the whole thing and lose your reputation [your job, the game, or whatever else is at stake]."

Faced with such an urgent situation, the Doubter grows alarmed, moving away from the Weakling and closer to the Critic. His alarming voice surfaces more frequently as the performance date draws closer (and can reach a pitch during the performance itself): "Look out! Watch it! Here comes the ball. Get under it. If you miss it, they'll think you're a fool." Or, "Your voice is too high. Get it down. Project. You've got phlegm in your throat, but don't cough—it'll spoil everything."

The messages can fly so fast they become a confused blur, which was the case with Joe. His thoughts were barely perceivable and flitted around in his head like a bat. One reason they flew so fast was that in the past, Joe had attempted to blot them out rather than try to decipher them. His blotting-out had worked so completely that at the very onset of the session, before envisioning the bat, he perceived nothing—no messages or images. His Doubter, with which he was identified, had gone a step beyond alarm to a state of confusion; the messages whirred around with such speed they outran his comprehension.

The first reaction of an individual in this state is to attempt to concentrate even harder (as recommended by the Dogmatist), but this compounds the problem. Struggling to force these fleeting messages into focus only ties the mind in a knot. All of us at some time have forgotten a person's name, and found that the harder we try to remember, the more the name escapes our tongue. Yet two seconds later, after we have released the stranglehold of concentration and diverted our attention elsewhere, the name clicks in our head. The answer to slips of memory and lack of concentration lies in partially loosening the reins on the thinking process and giving up stringent concentration.

Of course, the issue of confusion versus concentration is a major concern to performers, and some remedies to mend this internal split will be discussed later. But the initial step in resolving the conflict is to recognize which subpersonalities have been activated. If we feel confused, even if only a little, and this feeling is accompanied by a compulsion for restraint, this signals a probable transaction between the Doubter and the Dogmatist. Two possible inner dialogues might go something like this:

"I'm feeling confused."

"No, you can't be confused now. Concentrate harder."

Or, "What will happen if I can't remember my lines?"

"Stop doubting. You've got to watch every line."

In either case the Dogmatist pronounces infallible solutions for stagefright. Infallible or not, they usually—like most strong commands—provoke a response opposite the one intended.

Whenever we catch ourselves thinking in dogmatic terms, monitoring every action of a performance, or whenever we ask ourselves, "What will happen if . . . ," we are setting ourselves up for a Dogmatist/Doubter confrontation and we can be helped simply by watching these thoughts as an objective observer.

The Critic/Perfectionist

Although the Doubter and the Dogmatist wield a certain kind of power in the cluster, theirs is more or less an intellectual dominance—a stream of questions met with infallible answers. The real power in the stagefright group lies with the Critic, who by his prominence, strength, and hard-nosed messages is easily recognized. Like the Doubter, the Critic responds to mistakes, but the Doubter remains an uncertain skeptic wondering about the future. No skeptic, the Critic; he *knows* what will happen— the worst—and therefore keeps a scornful eye on the proceedings, mincing no words when something goes awry.

"Okay, kid. You blew it. If your opponent sees the backcourt is your weak spot, he's going to drive you back there and nail you. It was a stupid shot to miss."

We can remember that the Critic in his natural state is an assessor whose job is to point out weaknesses. His polar opposite, the Commender, points out strengths. Cut off from this polar interplay, however, the Critic turns cynical and begins to seek a mutated opposite, represented by the Perfectionist. These two share the same goal. They want an absolutely flawless performance. The Perfectionist represents the Critic's desire. If the Critic cries heatedly, "That was a stupid mistake," the Perfectionist counters with, "Don't get upset. Control yourself, or you'll make more mistakes." In short, the Critic knows what is "wrong" with a performance, the Perfectionist holds the "correct" answer to sort it out, and their energy is directly proportional. As the Critic's judgments become more accusatory and demeaning, the demands of the Perfectionist soar to unattainable heights. The Critic thus grows more frustrated, but against this the Perfectionist demands tighter control (to preserve his perfect character).

The Perfectionist's messages, like those of the Dogmatist, include such telltale expressions as "should," "have to," "ought," and "absolutely must." His most typical charge is that the performance must be absolutely flawless. If an action is less than correct, this stirs the Critic to describe it as "silly," "dumb," or "stupid." As a pair, their messages bristle with stinging authority.

An interesting pact between the two is found in the reward system to which they agree. Knowing that the Critic, in his natural state, seeks commendation for a job well done, the Perfectionist offers to reward the Critic if the performance is flaw-less—then the performer can feel worthy. But, as the Perfec-tionist told Joe, "If you don't play perfectly, you're no good." Playing flawlessly and being a worthy human being are linked here. Sometimes the reward is adulation, and the perfect per-formance is the one that thrills or astonishes the crowd. A performer who seeks this reward hankers after star status and as a result feels compelled to win at any cost, compete for every gain, and, in general, keep himself a step above everyone else. The catch, however, is that despite former successes, a per-formance is never quite good enough. The Critic thus is re-duced to a habitual cynic, groping for unattainable perfection.

We need to understand clearly that seeking unrealistic per-fection is quite different from having a healthy intent toward self-improvement. All of us need a sense of purpose to keep us directed toward maturity, and we set certain obtainable goals to accomplish this end. The goals of the Perfectionist, however, are unobtainable and result in greater frustration and uncer-tainty. Whenever we hold up an absolute, rigid standard to which we "must" measure up, we activate one part of ourselves that doubts our ability to meet the standard (the Doubter), and another part that grows irritated at our inability to do so. This latter part is the Critic, whose irritation festers until it reaches its zenith in full-blown anger.

Validating the Critic's anger, however, can produce stunning results. The following account is only one of many that shows something of what can happen when the performer validates the energy held by the Critic.

Jim, a private client, had a critical subpersonality like a bull-dozer. It could find fault with the very light of day, so you can imagine his Critic's comments about the way Jim played the piano. Jim himself was a very proper young man, always neatly dressed but shy and retiring. Consequently, when I suggested that he play for a few moments like a bulldozer, this made little sense to him. Still, he agreed to try and he then launched into a Beethoven sonata with a vengeance—head bent, arms flying. When he had finished, I asked for a reaction.

"Wow!" he said. "That felt good."

"Well, you certainly looked as if you were having fun. You may not want to play every piece that way, but it's good to know you have that energy available when you need it. By the way," I asked, "where is the stagefright you had ten minutes ago?"

"Uh, I guess it's gone," he said with a start.

The encounter had been quick and clean, and Jim found sensual pleasure in performing. Later in the session we talked about what might be getting in the way of this pleasure. Jim said that in the past, the strength he knew he possessed had created an inner threat, that somehow the feeling of power had stirred him to feel fear and embarrassment. With this realization, Jim hit upon a major factor in the stagefright issue—being afraid of one's own power in the stress of performing.

As we said at the very outset, performers approach an event with great enthusiasm when the date is comfortably in the distant future. As time draws near, however, uneasiness sets in, and the vigor with which we looked forward to performing turns to apprehension. The strength associated with the Critic does not find healthy expression, but is directed in the form of anger to a subpersonality who feels insecure. The anger of Jim's Critic was aimed at the Weakling and conjured up feelings of intimidation.

In a case like this, the Weakling, thus activated, takes over the cluster. The power structure is overturned; strength yields to weakness and excitement gives in to dread. The way in which the Weakling accomplishes this coup is a fascinating process and one that merits our detailed attention.

The Weakling/Protector

In examining the roles of the stagefright subpersonalities, we come to the most puzzling, yet intriguing pair of all—the Weakling and the Protector. According to the power structure of the cluster, this pair initially has no potency whatever and is subject to all the rest—especially to the Critic, who holds what we call the gut power of the group. Consequently, in the cluster's hierarchy this pair stands last in line. But there is an adage that says, The end of the road is wrought by the last in line. And, indeed, this is an apt description of the action of this devious duo; for somehow they manage to wrest control of the entire cluster through subversion. Although they wear a badge of ignorance and ineptitude, they spin a web of cunning strategy.

The Weakling in his natural state seeks a polar opposite of strength, available under normal circumstances from the Risker subpersonality. Denied this vigor from the other side, however, (because the Observing "I" is identified with stagefright) the Weakling feels victimized and seeks strength wherever he can find it. The most obvious source he can locate is the Critic, who has strength enough, but of the wrong kind for the Weakling, who needs sensitive encouragement. Accordingly, they are a mismatched pair, the one a cynic making sniping remarks, the other a victim beating retreat—but vowing retaliation.

In planning his strategy to cope with the Critic, the Weakling figures the smartest thing to do is play dumb, and in this he is the craftiest member of the cluster. He calculates that if he comes off as irresponsible and incompetent, others must do his work for him. He therefore will be free of responsibility and escape the Critic's wrath. So, when the Weakling hears accusations from the Critic, he throws up his hands in mock despair, lamenting his inability to measure up. The Weakling is a struggling dunce, it seems, caught by circumstances beyond his control.

To further his strategy, he seeks the aid of the Protector, who has a particular kind of strength not found in the Critic. While the Critic's strength is by nature offensive—vigorous and gutsy —that of the Protector is defensive—knotted and conniving— just the "right" mix to protect the Weakling's cover of ineptitude. His force is a bit like a sorcerer's, and with it he manages to cast a spell over all other subpersonalities, sending them scampering and leaving the Weakling unharmed. Seemingly, the power of the Protector stands in graphic contrast to the impotence of the Weakling, since his strength is like a "magic" power. His mettle is used to preserve impotence, however, so that neither he nor the Weakling can be held accountable. In this way, their self-esteem is preserved intact.

In casting his spell, the Protector emerges as a threatening figure, probably the most frightening of any subpersonality in the cluster. As a result, his image often assumes the form of a witch, reptile, or scary animal.*

In contrast, images of the Weakling might take the form of a cringing figure taunted by another subpersonality, even by the Protector himself. Sometimes animals indicate the Weakling, also. They are not scary animals, however, but rather ones who are themselves scared—two examples being a trembling puppy or a turtle hiding in his shell. More common than a frightened animal, though, is the image of a scared child running away or cowering in a corner.

Besides hearing inner cries for help and assigning great power to outside forces, however, one sure signal of our being identified with the Weakling is the way in which we respond to inner questions about our performance. The questions, we know, come from the Doubter, and if the Weakling is fielding them, each is met with a claim of ignorance.

"Are you ready for tomorrow's performance?"

---

*Scary animals present something of a puzzle in deciphering which subpersonality they represent, since these might symbolize any of the stagefright subpersonalities, except the Weakling. But they can be distinguished by the quality of energy they carry. For example, the angry Critic often is seen as a large beast, like a lion or tiger, whose energy is powerful. Occasionally, the alarmed Doubter surfaces as an agitated creature, like a fluttering bird or a bat (as in the account of Joe). Animals that represent the Protector, however, are drawn from the land of enchantment and loom as dragons, monsters, or demons. The energy they carry is unmistakably resentful and malicious.

"I don't know."

"What is the coach going to think?"

"Gee, I don't know."

"What will happen if you get off to a bad start?"

"Oh god, I don't know."

This litany serves to preserve the shield of ineptitude. It is true, of course, that for some of the Doubter's questions, we may have no ready answer. If "I don't know" runs through our thoughts like a tape loop, however, we can be sure the Weakling is at the switch.

There is another point to consider. The things we truly do not know with regard to our performance are surprisingly few. Very often we delude ourselves into "not knowing" by shrugging our shoulders in defeat, but there is something we fail to catch. After every "I don't know," there follows an unspoken "because." "I don't know, *because* ...."

We can learn a lot about the Weakling if we examine ourselves to see what information follows this key word. For example, we might say to ourselves, "I don't know *because* it's too much trouble to find out, or I'm scared to find out, or I'm too dumb to find out, or I don't *want* to find out."

One of the most frequent "I don't know" responses comes in answer to the question, "What will So-and-So think of my performance?" If we listen carefully to what comes after the "because," we might possibly hear something along these lines: "I don't know what So-and-So will think of my performance because I cannot control his mind—but I would certainly like to!"

Although rarely will such an answer be stated as frankly as this, it probably is hidden somewhere behind the Weakling's badge of ignorance, and it gives a hint of the character we have talked about before. On the surface he retreats from the demands of the Critic and the questions of the Doubter, but in actuality he seeks domination. The way in which he seeks to control others (subpersonalities, or persons) is by claiming to be out of control and drawing them to the rescue. They must save him from his "uncontrolled" state. Yet his manipulations must be guarded, for if others guessed the truth, his ruse would be ended and his peculiar power lost. To this end he engages the talents of the Protector, who by casting a spell enables the Weakling to wrest control of the cluster.

CHAPTER 5

Stagefright
and Protective Maneuvers

IN ORDER TO APPRECIATE THE FULL FORCE of the Protector, we need to investigate not only the voice he creates in us, but also the protective maneuvers he influences us to take with the hope of overcoming stagefright. More aptly these maneuvers are the devices he employs to defend the Weakling. Frequently the pact between the Weakling and the Protector is unspoken. At first the Protector uses a subtle defense wherein the stagefright subpersonalities chat among themselves fairly freely. When subtlety fails, however, more drastic ploys are called into service. Finesse gives in to deceit, so that by turns the subpersonalities grow silent, reaching a point where the voices of stagefright escape detection. Consequently, we consider the voice of the Protector in the context of his devices and these we can divide into two categories, according to the impact they carry: first, his subtle tactics, and second, his more sophisticated sly tricks.

SUBTLE TACTICS

One of the subtle tactics the Protector engages in is the face-saving apology, manufactured to cover the Weakling's embarrassment. This is how it works.

A junior executive has labored for a week getting a report ready for presentation and it is now complete. Although he has put forth his best effort in organizing the material, he still hears the voices of his inner directors—the Doubter asking what the boss is going to think, the Critic telling him the boss is going to tear it apart, and the Perfectionist prescribing things that remain to be done to make it perfect. All of these are heard by the Weakling who grows progressively uneasy as the appointed hour draws nigh. In reaction to the Weakling's call, the Protector comes to the rescue, and just as the report is about to be given, he announces for all to hear, "I didn't get a chance to organize the report the way I'd like. This week has been a real bear."

Not only does this tactic protect the Weakling from the demands of the power group, it alerts the audience not to expect too much and, therefore, not to judge too harshly. Using this tactic, the Protector saves the day. The unspoken promise, however—and one that is lost for the moment—is that the speaker has committed himself to be better organized, next time. Consequently, when the next time comes the stakes seem higher, the Critic speaks louder, and the necessity for saving face is greater. However, as the need for defense grows, so do explanations multiply. As a result, the face-saving apology expands (let's get down to brass tacks) into an "ass-saving" excuse. Such excuses seem to come in threes. Thus, before the next report, the original apology may expand to these dimensions: I'm sorry, etc., etc. (1) This week was a real bear. (2) I was out for a day with the flu, and (3) I didn't get the material until yesterday.

Generally, apologies and excuses begin almost off-handedly,

but since they stave off stagefright temporarily, they become a habit. At the same time, they carry the claim that the performer is more capable than his present showing demonstrates, a claim for which next time he will be held accountable. Therefore, in addition to being habit forming, they are addictive; each dose requires a bigger pill. Not only that, as the excuses grow in scope, it becomes more and more apparent they are based on false premises. The embarrassment they were intended to cover grows a bit more intense, turning into guilt.

Guilt, of course, complicates the problem. An individual who feels guilty, feels also ashamed—unworthy of commendation. Thus, if any kind word comes from a member of the audience, the only seeming recourse for the individual is to turn the compliment away. Hence, the Protector engages in the "compliment discount" to blot out the good wish. Most compliment discounts begin with the phrase, "Thank you, but . . . ."

"Thank you, but I could have been much better organized if I had had more time." Or, "Thank you, but you should have seen the dress rehearsal. It was much better."

A compliment discount wields three punches. First, it attempts to dispel guilt for a subpar performance, explaining that things usually go much better. In addition, it tells the well-wisher that the performer holds vast reserves of talent and ability awaiting fruition under the right conditions. (What these might be is usually left unclear.) The real punch, however, is its subtle attack on the bearer of praise. It acts as a put-down, silently informing the compliment-giver that he or she has shown bad judgment in praising a substandard performance. Thus quashed, the compliment-giver is kept at safe distance, lest he penetrate the cover. Cover or no, the ruse prevails and, along with it, a stronger sense of guilt.

Because the Weakling is left with more guilt, he may call upon the Protector to dispel it another way—by pawning it off on someone else, in what is known as the "guilt slough." This device may be called into play when apologies, excuses, and discounts no longer quell the jitters; in such a case, the report-giver just mentioned may attempt to blame someone else for his lack of organization.

"The boss," he says, letting himself off the hook, "has such a 'hang-up' for petty detail. How can I give a decent report with him breathing down my neck?"

Almost anyone can be the target of a guilt slough: teachers ("My teacher makes me nervous because he looks for every mistake"), teammates ("John is going to be watching every move I make, because he wants my place in the starting lineup"), even the whole audience ("You never can count on an audience these days, they're all so fickle"). Not only that, situations or objects can be equally to blame: "The acoustics in here are against me." In all these cases, something outside the performer is seen to carry the cause for impeding the performance.

The same is true with the other "tactics," too—they all work in conjunction with the perception that the threat comes from outside. But this is only the outer transaction. The real encounter involves triple feedback between members of the upper and lower cluster. A member of the power group (most likely the Critic) denounces the Weakling, who, feeling embarrassed or guilty, calls on the Protector, who undermines the Critic, and the cycle begins again.

The solution to stopping this merry-go-round is to pull the plug. We can give up making excuses (which probably are more habit than design). We can stop blaming others for our self-imposed jitters and assume full responsibility for our performance, whatever the outcome. When we receive a kind word for a job well done, we can accept the compliment graciously: "Thank you. I worked hard on the project and I appreciate your good wishes."

It all seems quite simple, yet, because the Protector's methods are based on various habits of thought, the solution is far easier to describe in words than to carry out in action. The way we think is difficult to change, indeed. Without change, however, the merry-go-round whirls faster and faster, and the Protector's methods grow still more sophisticated. Subtle tactics are replaced by sly tricks.

SLY TRICKS

Sly tricks, like subtle tactics, are an attempt to exempt the performer from living up to his or her potential, but in practice they carry more clout. The first of these tricks is cynical humor.

"It'd be just like me to miss the last shot of a tied game. Ha, ha." Or, "I can just see myself playing perfectly and missing the last chord of the piece. I'll probably fall flat on my face trying to get off stage. Ho, ho, ho."

Not only does this brand of humor let the performer off the hook, it also provides the Weakling with some longed-for attention. Persons who hear the witty lines above will be prompted to pat the jester on the back, saying, "Good old George. He's such a clown. Always good for a chuckle. Heh, heh."

Even though the jester lets himself off one hook, however, he fashions another that is sharper. He sets himself up to blunder exactly as he predicted because of the interaction between subpersonalities. The "good" humor above stems from the Protector and alerts all the subpersonalities in the power cluster to be on guard. They converge on the spot in question (the last shot, the final chord), hoping to avoid catastrophe. When the performer arrives at the point in question, they give their full attention to the situation, focusing all their energy on it. With all this energy converging on one spot, the system overloads. The performer's mind goes blank and the jester finds himself in a self-fulfilling prophecy.

The step beyond cynical humor is cold-blooded spite. A performer playing this trick secretly rejoices in the misfortunes of his or her colleagues in order to bolster a teetering self-concept. "It serves her right to fail. She hasn't worked hard enough to deserve success." (Meaning, "She hasn't suffered the way I have.")

Success of the trick requires upstaging one's professional rivals in some way, or perhaps dropping devious comments about another performer's fallibility. Clawing for recognition by playing tricks of the trade is a fraudulent game, and we must distinguish it from honest hard work in which the fruits of success are won (or lost) by fair play.

Without a doubt, the most deceitful (and dangerous) trick played by the Protector is one in which he encourages the performer to overcome the jitters of stagefright by taking stress-reducing drugs. Tranquilizers and alcohol anesthetize the Critic, blotting out his demands so that the Protector need not work so hard. With the inner crossfire deadened, the performer is left free to perform without libel. But it is a freedom leading to bondage, a trick destined to fail.

The taking of drugs is unfortunately a widespread practice among some performers and is, in fact, sanctioned in certain quarters of the medical profession. One such drug, oxprenolol, has been used experimentally to treat stagefright in musicians, surgeons, race-car drivers, pilots, and public speakers* In technical terms, the drug blocks the beta-adrenergic division of the nervous system—the part that responds to perceived threats by producing an overwhelming rush of energy. This means the drug checks those physical responses to stagefright such as tremors, rapid heartbeat, and high blood pressure, but does not affect the entire nervous system as do older types of tranquilizers.

Because the drug works peripherally, rather than centrally over the whole system, some hail oxprenolol as a possible breakthrough in the treatment of stagefright. That may be. But the root cause of stagefright will remain untouched, since its solution is grounded in self-awareness and self-concept, which, in

---

*See I. M. James and others, "Effect of Oxprenolol on Stagefright in Musicians," *Lancet* (Nov. 5, 1977), pp. 952–54; Samuel Vaisrub, "Pursuit of 'Eucardia,'" *Journal of the American Medical Association* (Oct. 28, 1978), p. 1893.

our terminology, depends on the subpersonalities with which an individual identifies himself or herself. Although the drug muzzles the cries of the Critic and the Weakling, it in no way signs their truce, nor does it satisfy any questions concerning self-identity.

Two Kinds of Fear

Throughout all the foregoing tactics and tricks, we find a common thread that binds the Weakling and Protector together—the concealment of vulnerability. The so-called necessity for hiding our vulnerable state is fed by two specific kinds of fear. One is the fear of defeat, the other, the fear of accomplishment. Feeding on these fears is the means by which the Weakling wins over the cluster. He succeeds with panic rather than power, enticing or scaring the other subpersonalities into submission. And to add the final touch, whether it be the fear of failure or the fear of success, either way, fear is the victor.

The Fear of Failure

Most of us see the fear of failure as stemming from some past catastrophe we would just as soon forget, but this is not always the case. The fear of failure is often predicated on past *successes*. We can recall the coach of the National Cyclones, whom we talked about earlier. When he identified himself simply as the coach, his internal Critic served him well. It told him how to coach, direct, and guide the team—so well, in fact, that he had a winning streak. However, when he changed his identification to that of the winning coach who must sustain his string of victories, this new alignment brought increased demands from his Critic.

Winning from the Critic's point of view entailed greater perfection, more controls, and higher expectations, and these he passed on to the Weakling. As the Critic's demands grew more rigid, the Weakling depleted more of the Critic's strength in order to build up fear. Consequently, with each new demand, the Critic grew more threatened. For the coach, each new win brought higher stakes, and with higher stakes came bigger threats: each win thus increased the fear of failure.

In terms of subpersonalities, we can describe the setup behind the fear of failure as a tug-of-war between the Critic and the Weakling. The Critic, embodying the desires for perfection and control, possesses a hammer-like strength that, when frustrated, turns to anger. Holding such strength, he hopes to pry the Weakling out of his cowering corner and prod him into some course of action. The Weakling, however, embraces the opposite qualities, those of helplessness, defensive protection, guilt, embarrassment, and, of course, fear. These energies are *re*active in nature.

As the reactive entity, the Weakling is the receiver of the Critic's energy, and his goal is to maintain the status quo, soaking up the Critic's power. In order to keep the energy flowing his way he meets the Critic's demands either with no response or with a claim of inadequacy. Thus, the more energy the Critic pours out, the more energy the Weakling absorbs. As the Critic's charges grow more strident, so the pangs of fear grow in kind. If this transaction continues unaltered, and all the Critic's energy becomes exhausted, the Weakling, with his usurped strength, overcomes the Critic, who sinks back, giving up the cause.

The Fear of Success

Although most performers admit to the fear of failure, few recognize the opposite phantom—the fear of success. Whereas the fear of failure arises from a conflict between the Critic and the Weakling, the fear of success is spawned by the Weakling and the Protector. In the first case, the Weakling is afraid he will not live up to the demands of the Critic; in the second, he fears he might do just that. Moreover, if he were to succeed, he would exceed his sense of self and this he resists. To an outside observer such an attitude seems absurd, but in a curious way, it is understandable.

Expanding one's self-concept entails undertaking new experiences, the outcome of which cannot be predicted. This spells risk. Not only that, if one were successful in expanding one's self-concept, this would involve maintaining the newly acquired state. And this means meeting the higher standards as well as assuming greater responsibilities. Therefore, keeping the status quo, despite its limitations and its twisted perception, is more comfortable than finding success, because the present condition is familiar, and from familiarity one knows what to expect.

The fact that any of us might fear success may be hard to swallow, but this fear's voice is familiar to all when it comes as a whisper in the middle of performance; "This is going so well. It can't last. You haven't even made a mistake." Or, "Ten free throws in a row—right in the basket. You're only a 60 percent shooter. You can't do this."

Some performers report that when a performance is going extremely well, beyond their expectations, they tremble more than ever. To counteract this dreadful feeling, they sometimes make a mistake intentionally so they can say to themselves, "Okay, now that I've botched it, I can relax and get on with the performance." By this, they maintain the status quo of a mediocre (but comfortable) performance.

More specifically, it is the Protector who maintains the status quo. He protects the Weakling against success by devising subtle schemes to keep the Weakling within his limited self-concept. On the surface, all the earlier subtle tactics and sly tricks are presumed to protect self-esteem, but their real intent is to *destroy* self-esteem, since they all serve to keep the Weakling weak, and the Protector strong. Although they propose to reduce stagefright, they actually strengthen its grasp. If an individual engages in face-saving devices, the face he saves is that of the limited concept of self as perceived by the Weakling. If the performer should happen to succeed, the Weakling and Protector would then lose their uncanny power in the cluster.

TRAPS OF FAULTY PREPARATION

There is one final device of the Protector that needs mentioning and we do so here, since it is more directly related to the fear of success than the earlier schemes first indicate. We can call this last device the trap of faulty preparation, since it is more trap than trick, and it is sprung in three different ways.

One setup of the trap might be called the low-stakes design. Here, the Protector tells the Weakling that the demands for quality are lower than usual. Maybe the event is old hat by now; perhaps the audience or the city is less than prestigious, or the competition weaker than before. Because the stakes seem low, the event is viewed without much concern. Let's say a quarterback has played several tough games in a row, but is about to face a team considered to be a pushover. The Protector might explain the situation in these terms: "Look, the last three games have been stingers, but next week's is a snap. No problem. It's a second-rate team." Next week rolls around and because of overconfidence the team loses. But the Weakling, aided by the Protector, wins.

Another method of setting the trap (this one more stealthy than the low-stakes approach) is what we might call the stuck design. Here, the Weakling has trouble overcoming inertia. He delays starting his preparation or, after starting it, sputters distractedly along by fits and starts until the deadline is breathing down his neck. Rather than giving attention to necessary preparation, he is lured into pursuing other ends, sometimes totally unrelated to the matter at hand. To illustrate, a history professor is scheduled to give a lecture on "The Roosevelt Years," and for one reason or another, becomes identified with his Weakling. While struggling through his historical research, a random thought begins to tickle his fancy. For many years he has intended reading the entire works of Shakespeare and now, mysteriously, he craves to do just that, even though Shakespeare is worlds apart from Roosevelt. An inner voice from the Protector beckons, "You never have time to do what you really want. How nice it would be to settle in by the fire with a bowl of chestnuts and *A Winter's Tale*, rather than hammering away on Roosevelt." Remarkably, this long-time craving never made a peep during the professor's vacation!

The last trap of faulty preparation is related to the one above in that it also works to scatter the performer's attention. This setup is the overbooked design, wherein the performer overcrowds his agenda. He schedules too many events too close together so that inevitably he is too tired to perform his best. He may even get sick. Overbooking, however, provides certain rewards. For one, it gives the performer the excuse of being too busy to prepare adequately. For another, it provides the feeling of being in demand, which many seem to need. In addition, it presents for some performers a certain kind of challenge to prevail despite the overbooked schedule. This last may seem particularly enticing, since meeting challenges is one means of measuring success. But meeting challenges is one thing; overcoming self-imposed obstacles is another. If a performer has crowded his schedule to the point where his showing is affected, he is not meeting challenges but falling into a trap—one set by the Protector and calculated for failure. When the failure comes, the Weakling can sink back with a sigh of relief, explaining, "But look how hard I tried."

With this remark we come to the basic conclusion found in all the schemes we have discussed. When we think back over the excuses, apologies, traps of faulty preparation, and all the other protective maneuvers, we realize that this remark, whether spoken or not, is the hidden dynamic with which the Weakling accomplishes his purpose. In the end when all the dust has settled, he can sink back and sigh, "But look how hard I tried." This is how he exempts himself from blame, how he conceals his vulnerability. In short, this is how he wins.

We know, of course, that each time he exempts himself accordingly, this stirs up greater fear whenever the next occasion arises. Yet this also is how he wins. This is how he takes over the stagefright cluster of subpersonalities, by creating the fear that brings them to submission. In other words, he wins by sabotage. Furthermore, his sabotage is bound to triumph, for no matter the outcome—whether our performance succeeds or fails—fear prevails.

Still, there is a paradox here and it presents the turning point in our investigation. The fear held by the Weakling is only an outer shell, a cover for something else inside. Beneath the fear lies a quality utterly different from the outside shell. Moreover, we can say the same with respect to the other stagefright subpersonalities. Each of them possesses an intrinsic quality that is in some way valuable to our performance, somehow enriching to the occasion. Behind all their messages and maneuvers are found the souls of the Critic, the Doubter, and the Weakling. To find these inner souls, however, we must enter into the feelings that propel them. When we discover their inner emotions, their voices are transformed of their own accord.

CHAPTER 6

Stagefright and Feelings

Emotional activity in the stagefright cluster presents the most difficult area for the performer to examine, because emotions, more than thought patterns, tend to pull the performer off-center from the position of the Observing "I." Wrapped up in the exigency of a forthcoming event, the performer is apt to be carried away in a flood of emotions with which he or she is closely identified. Yet despite that, the feelings carry the answer. Beneath their outward threat lies an intrinsic quality that can guide the performer in his or her purpose.

A hint about the nature of the core qualities can be gathered if we return to the concept of polar opposites. If we weigh the abstract concept of *emotion*, collectively speaking, against its opposite, we can say that the polarity to emotion is a state of *nonemotion*. Nonemotion implies an attitude of indifference or detachment. Had we no feelings regarding a particular event, we would have no concern about it. All emotions show an element of concern, a basic measure of sensitivity; otherwise, none of them would come to life.

Thus the primary emotions in the stagefright cluster—anger, fear, and confusion—although seemingly conflicting and detrimental to the occasion, are born out of an inner affection for and attraction to the performing experience. Without affinity for performance, we would have no feelings toward that end— no stagefright beforehand (and no elation afterwards). At the core of stagefright lies a kernel of fascination, an attraction and a commitment to performing.

But how does commitment arise from such seemingly malignant feelings as anger, fear, and confusion?

In looking for the answer, let us again recall the simple polarity of hot versus cold, which we discussed earlier. We said that warm, the integrated quality between the opposites, contains elements of both hot and cold. The reverse, however, is just as valid. Hot and cold each contain the quality of warm (since any temperature level above absolute zero contains at least a measure of heat). Warm, therefore, is the core quality shared by each.

To get to the core energies of the specific feelings in the stagefright cluster, we can think in terms of particular emotional polarities—not the broad polarity of feelings versus nonfeelings, but narrower ones that distinguish specific emotional dichotomies, in our case the respective polarities of anger, fear, and confusion. By considering these feelings, their respective polar opposites, and their subsequent integration, we can arrive at the core energy of each and see the real essence behind the feelings of stagefright. As hinted earlier, perhaps the feeling that offers the most unexpected dividend is anger.

ANGER

On some occasion you may have been offended at the way a friend treated you, but from fear of upsetting the friendship you said nothing about the infraction. With nothing said, your feelings mount until they threaten to explode. If you and your friend agree to talk about the way you feel, you may start with an attack, accusing him or her of being selfish and insensitive to your feelings. In this stage your energy is that of strong aggression. You have your say and get the matter off your chest. Afterwards, you have a sense of release, and feel strangely calm inside. In a quiet voice you then tell your friend that the reason you got angry is that you felt hurt and excluded. To this, the friend may respond with something like, "Gee, I didn't know I had hurt you," or, "Well, you do some things that hurt me, too." After a few similar exchanges you might ask, "What can we do to stop hurting each other?" and add, "I value your friendship." At this point the bond between you begins to mend and you feel a new closeness for that individual. In the end a new alliance is effected, and a metamorphosis of feelings has taken place—from wrath to release, and from release to reconciliation.

For our purposes this transformation of feelings can be explained in this way: anger (once expressed) has as its polarity a temper of calmness we can label "tranquility." The union of these extremes creates a higher entity we can call "compassion," for it possesses a kind of glowing reconciliation. The metamorphosis, then, involves three interrelated states: anger, tranquility, and compassion.

Although these states may appear to have little in common, we can get a better idea of their alliance if we refer back to the hot-cold polarity. Remembering the earlier explanation, that the core essence of the extremes is found in the union of the two, we realize that the core of anger is in fact compassion. Thus compassion is the ultimate quality revealed when anger is honestly expressed. A total transformation occurs, gathering momentum as it evolves.

To clarify the meaning of compassion as used here we can distinguish it from the feelings of pity or sympathy. These latter two are couched in a missionary tone of rescue and protection. That is to say, if we feel pity for someone, we are apt to excuse their faults, look after their needs, and in general protect them from unpleasantness—all of which suggest the Protector. Compassion is different. If we feel compassion for another, we feel love, to be sure, but not blind attachment. We do not excuse their errors or attempt to rescue them from adversity, but with affection we deal openly with their shortcomings. Compassion is not an attitude of tea and sympathy, but one of *active caring* that sometimes expresses itself in anger.

How does all this relate to stagefright? As we have said, our outward transactions mirror our inner thoughts and feelings. Every performer experiencing stagefright feels a threat to identity, and with that threat—whether he or she is aware of it— comes a certain degree of anger. Anger created by stagefright seeks the same resolution as that just described, with the difference being that the transaction goes on internally and does not necessarily come out of our mouths (though it certainly may). Nevertheless, whether in our heads or out of our mouths, anger longs to contact its natural polar opposite, tranquility, and express its core entity, compassion. What keeps this from happening is the performer himself.

As explained before, the performer behind the block of stagefright cannot see anger's polar opposite on the other side and senses only the outer threat. That performer fails also to see that tranquility is available if anger is released and, consequently, holds on to his or her present feelings. Denied its natural polarity, the anger shifts into a kind of quiet rage that is even more threatening—if temper is lost, the performer risks losing control of the situation (figure 6.1).

In assuming that control provides the answer for his or her dilemma, the performer mistakes control for tranquility. The error is not totally without justification, since the latter possesses an element of cool objectivity. Although the terms are remotely related, they are not interchangeable. Control is a part of tranquility, but the control in tranquility is of a richer variety and more flexible than its distant "cousin." We might describe

Figure 6.1. Anger Matrix

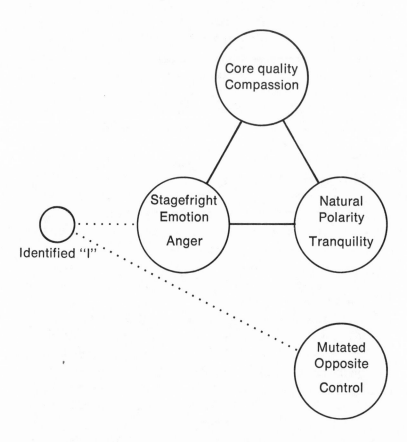

tranquility as a state of energetic calmness, an attitude of vibrant composure. It displays a kind of settled strength in which calmness is impregnated with enthusiam.

The control sought from the mutated variety conveys unflinching restraint, whereby thoughts, feelings, or actions are forced into submission. Thus tranquility, and not control, is the quality performers seek, for with it one is free to guide his or her energies, rather than being bound to stifle them. Moreover, tranquility is the natural polarity to anger. Whereas control increases the polar split, tranquility allows the split to be mended.

Anger and tranquility share a bond of mutual dependence. Anger looks for resolution. It seeks guidance, for without that, its energy would dissipate into impotent rage. Tranquility, on the other hand, seeks the energy of anger as a source of strength; otherwise it would mutate into lethargy. Thus the opposites contribute to each other. One gives guidance, the other power, and with their mutual sharing they merge into the higher entity we call compassion.

Compassion, of course, is an excellent answer for stagefright, but let us remember that anger is a part of the larger entity. We can use the energy of anger not only to dissipate fear, but also to bring about a higher commitment to performance. It is a commitment that evolves from our inner encouragement toward excellence, one that differs markedly from the kind of duty-driven struggle that springs from a lack of self-esteem. This latter setup is advocated by the Perfectionist and takes us on a rocky road to success.

Finding a renewed sense of commitment by expressing honest anger always brings a sense of delight. Recall the account of Jim, the proper pianist. When he chose to brave anger as an experiment, he had fun and found a new dimension in his playing. Formerly, his anger had been held in (inwardly directed from the Critic to the Weakling), and he was afraid of it, lest he completely lose his senses.

Anger habitually suppressed can often become stultifying criticism. Rather than risk being angry, we turn instead to the safer ground of self-censure. We thus may be well aware of our inner Critic; we may hear his voice, yet be oblivious to the emotion he carries. Denied an avenue of release, the energy seeks expression elsewhere. Our inward criticism seeps out as attacks on others. Therefore, the performer who constantly criticizes others or consistently finds circumstances below par can suspect that anger plays a large part in his stagefright cluster.

Inwardly directed anger may be caused by feelings of unworthiness or some seeming lack of preparation, but more often than not, anger is caused by fear. Performers become angry with themselves for being scared. Yet, bottling anger builds fear and covering fear increases anger. The trapped energy needs to be released; one needs to find a way to express the feelings of anger *by choice*, before the fury reaches volcanic proportions.

By experiencing anger and letting go of its tension, we find in its stead a totally different power, a commitment toward performance characterized by a warmth of affection.

Finding such qualities in the block of stagefright seems beyond reason (and in a way it is, since emotions provide the vehicle), yet in addition to these, the block holds equally valuable resources at the core of the other stagefright feelings.

FEAR

Although most performers about to face an audience rarely perceive any hint of holding anger, they do know with certainty the fear they feel. We considered fear in the last chapter, in which we spoke mainly about its threat to the Weakling and its subsequent effect upon the Protector. Here, however, we want to go beyond the outer threat to the core essence of fear, which can guide the performer in his or her purpose. We need to look at the feeling itself, and see if we can determine what its inner sensations suggest.

In considering the inner sensations of fear, perhaps we can best describe it in contrast to anger in terms of energy. When we vent anger, there is a feeling of strength, expansion, and warmth. Fear, on the contrary, stimulates the sensations of weakness, contraction, and frigidity. It seems as if the energy of fear hides itself. There is a feeling of being exposed, vulnerable, and on the brink of danger that brings with it the possibility of hurt and humiliation.

Perhaps you remember a time before a performance when you felt like hiding and would have given anything to find relief from those queasy feelings. Maybe to bolster your courage you diligently reminded yourself that by any rational standard you had nothing to fear. Failing that, perhaps you tried positive thinking, but found this impossible (since thinking good thoughts is difficult to do if one is on the verge of regurgitating). Still failing to find relief, maybe you tried to steel yourself by controlling all your feelings. But nothing seemed to work. Finally, by curtain time, with all your efforts exhausted, you simply said to yourself, as if diving from a high board, "Well, here goes." Then you took the plunge, giving yourself up to whatever might happen. Curiously, though you are not sure exactly how, the performance clicked. Afterwards you felt joyously exuberant, wondering why you felt such pangs of uncertainty beforehand. This transformation of feelings gives a clue to the nature of fear, its natural polarity, and its core essence.

In the example just cited, the shift of feelings began with the decision to give ourselves up and take the plunge. That decision marked the first step toward courage, giving in to fear. When that happened, the energy of fear began to tap into the energy of courage. Gradually, as these polarities began to merge, a sense of joy burst into bloom. Admittedly, the decision to give in to fear was in this case made as a last resort, almost out of desperation. But the performer does not have to wait until the situation becomes so desperate. Early on, an individual can choose to trust his or her preparation and accept whatever happens in the performance. In this way the performer "connects" with the energy of courage and does so by conscious choice. Without the courage to greet fear, however, he or she seeks a mutated solution, desiring a kind of blind confidence to dissipate fear (figure 6.2).

Blind confidence is a reward promised—but never delivered—by the Protector; and since it is, it carries many shades of meaning. Sometimes, performers hope to gain the reward by engaging in guilt sloughs and other tactics associated with the Protector. Other times, they believe that the reward might be found

Figure 6.2. Fear Matrix

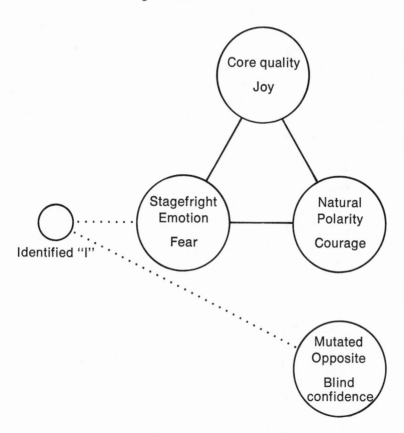

in a kind of magic button and reason to themselves: "If only I were two feet taller than the other players, if only I had three more weeks, if only the hall were better—*then* I would be confident."

Blind confidence is viewed as something that everyone else possesses, except us. It seems to exist somewhere "out there" just beyond our grasp—*if only* we knew the magic button to push. The answer to fear, however, is not found in a magic button, but in courage—courage to give in to the fear.

Some might wonder, though, what happens if we give in to the fear and the performance falls apart? By all odds, this is unlikely to happen if the performer is adequately prepared both professionally and physically. Making the decision to give in to fear and trust one's preparation is a way to enter the block—to look fear in the eye and thus begin to transform its energy. When the performer is well prepared and trusts his or her preparation, he or she will in all probability give an exciting and pleasurable performance. It may not be one of absolute perfection, meeting the unrealistic demands of an inner Perfectionist, but it will be one of authenticity, wherein the performer approaches the height of his or her capabilities. Accepting the fear silences the stagefright subpersonalities. If the decision is made to trust and accept whatever happens, they have nothing to talk about. Thus we can conclude that if their voices persist, we have declined to accept fear.

If we try to fight fear or run away from it, we begin to feel a sense of panic; but something else evolves if we give in to its energy by choice. We give up our *fear* of fear. Accepting fear constitutes the courage part of the polarity. This is the way fear is changed—not by a gruelling determination to overcome it, but by the willing agreement to embrace it. With that, the energy is transformed.

What value will be revealed cannot be predicted, but we can recall the outcome of an earlier account to see the process in action. Frank, the lawyer, you will remember, had a fear of trembling when he stood before an audience. During the workshop, he accepted that fear by vehemently shaking the paper he read for the group. Simply being willing to risk shaking before the group was his first step toward courage. Not only that, he found good humor in dramatizing and exaggerating the situation, because when he did, he found that this behavior had existed only in his mind as a preconceived fantasy. He feared the fantasy of coming apart, but when he chose to do so, it simply did not happen. He had, in his words, "trouble getting the paper to shake." In giving credence to his fear, its energy was transformed.

Two similar experiences involving speakers also come to mind. At another workshop, a social worker expressed concerns almost parallel to those of the lawyer. He feared trembling hands and a quavering voice, and told the group he felt almost like hiding while speaking to an audience. Thus, for the workshop he experimented with hiding from the group and made an impromptu speech from behind a pile of chairs stacked so high he had to strain to see over it. Gradually, as he began to grasp the physical barrier he had set up, he realized that in the past he had hidden from the audience psychologically, by making his voice weak. Seeing that the physical barrier was unrealistic, he decided to find out what would happen if he took it down. So, one by one, he began to dismantle the pile of chairs, and with each chair he removed, his voice grew stronger. As it did, he felt more "connected" with the group and they, him.

Had he not gone through the experience, he would have continued to intellectualize about what was wrong with his performance and would have continued to concentrate on controlling his shaking hands and quavering voice. What was wrong was not so much a case of the shakes, although that was there, but rather his feeling of isolation, one he had set up for himself. His solution lay not in controlling his hands and voice, but in risking to reach out to his audience. But no one could have explained the solution in words. (Perhaps some readers have been told to forget themselves in performance and think about whatever it is that they mean to communicate, only to discover they either cannot do so or do not know how.) By *experiencing* the barrier, however, this performer was able to dismantle it and gain strength in the process. With future talks he could choose to recall this experience mentally and, through his imagination, disassemble the barrier whenever he spoke.

On another occasion a workshop participant presented an even more graphic tableau. She spoke to the group as a "turtle," because that was her picture of fear, a tightly drawn knot covered by a shell that grew heavier as she talked. In the past she had not wanted to face the audience, so this time she did not. She drew her body into a ball, with her head hidden between her knees. Upon giving herself the freedom *not* to face the audience, she, like the social worker, discovered her isolated and cut-off position. With graphic awareness and acceptance of that stance, she began to wonder if exposure might offer a better alternative for her. With the decision to risk exposure to the audience, she gave herself permission to lift the shell. As she mimed lifting off the covering, her hunched-over posture slowly unfolded. Her head and upper torso moved gracefully upward. With fascination she exclaimed, "Wow. I feel so tall!"

Symbolically she had passed through the shadow and had emerged with a new sense of expandedness. By experiencing fear, she had moved to the other side and discovered a renewed sense of courage. In fact, she felt more than courage. It was a feeling of dynamism, vigor, and effervescence—in sum, a sense of joy.

From all three accounts we get a clearer idea about the quality at the core of fear, its nature, and the means by which it is discovered. All three individuals found behind the shell of fear an inner substance of joy, and each found it by entering into and experiencing the fear they felt. No one can forecast precisely, or describe accurately, the quality to be discovered. For some it carries a tone of joviality; for others, a hint of awesomeness. But for all, it is a sense of adventure that brings with it the opportunity for inner growth.

Such an opportunity to grow contrasts sharply with the requirement to excel. One is natural and stimulating; the other, forced and stultifying. Yet often the two concepts are confused and fear is perceived not as a way toward natural growth, but as a means to achieve artificial motivation.

It is true that fear can serve as a motivator and, if used wisely, can help performers channel their energies into a course of action. All too often, however, performers use fear not as a true motivator, but as a threat to whip themselves into shape. This is the method used by the inner Critic. Unfortunately, the same tactic is used by many authority figures—teachers, employers, coaches, and the like—who attempt to scare the performer into excelling. Some describe this tactic more euphemistically as the need to "psych up" for a performance. Fear used in this way results in noncreativity, a lack of experimentation, and dependence on others for ideas and motivation. Inner stimulation is stifled. Inertia sets in and the performer does nothing until threatened. He or she procrastinates and dawdles through the day until a deadline closes in or an angry boss goads that person into action. Thus, the individual returns to the familiar treadmill, feeling threatened and abused.

As we have seen, feeling threatened is the touchstone of stagefright, and perceiving a threat stirs the forces of fear as well as those of anger. Although the energy of both fills the performer, neither is expressed, because the power at the other side remains untapped. The performer, rather than accepting the energy and releasing its bond, holds it trapped inside, where it festers and becomes a state of confusion. Trapped energy, then, best describes the third emotion in the stagefright cluster, confusion.

CONFUSION

Although the energy in confusion is trapped, it comprises a composite emotion, midway between anger and fear and having traits of both. There is a tremendous force in confusion similar to that of anger, and, at the same time, a cowering dread similar to that of fear. Neither, however, is expressed. We almost could say that confusion is a *mutated* integration of anger and fear, when their energy is bottled up.

Often, confusion is in effect the first emotion performers feel with the first inkling of stagefright. First of all, they are uncertain about the outcome of their performance, but, more important, they are unclear about what is happening inside them-selves—unaware of their anger and unaccepting of their fear.

In defining how confusion feels in our bodies, we can speak of a spinning quality. "My head is spinning" graphically pic-tures the inner state of confusion. That statement demonstrates the way in which confusion differs from the other two emo-tions. Anger and fear are emotions bred in the bone, dwelling in the pit of the stomach, whereas confusion is more of the head. In fact, it is an intellectualized emotion, one that seeks to suppress the gut reactions. Consequently, the inner feel of confusion is one of indecision, an impulse to fly in every direc-tion yet travel in none, like an automobile spinning its wheels.

Though confusion possesses vast amounts of energy, all is trapped or wasted in an effort to hold back anger and cover up fear. When this energy is released, we find that confusion also holds a valuable resource at its core, one that can lead the per-former to new insights concerning his or her performance.

We can get a good idea about this intrinsic quality at the core of confusion if we consider a simple analogy: confusion is like a five-hundred-piece puzzle we want to assemble. On our first look at the jumbled pile, we wonder if we ever will get all the tiny bits together. The job seems overwhelming until we begin to examine the pieces more closely and find two or three that go together. The pace is quite slow, and we know if we attempt to speed up the process, we run the risk of forcing to-gether pieces that do not fit. This does not mean we dawdle, for our progress is full of purpose and intent. We know a solu-tion is forthcoming, and step by step the puzzle seems to fall into place. Confusion implies that there is an answer to the problem, even though we have not as yet unscrambled it.

The first step in finding an answer is to acknowledge the quandary of confusion. By experiencing confusion, we begin to focus our attention on it, and that allows us to examine the problem further. Accordingly, we can label the polarity of con-fusion as being a state of focus. Just as with other polarities we have discussed, focus and confusion play off each other. Confusion longs for focus, but we cannot know focus without knowing confusion. Focus here implies that the energy of confusion, which is directionless, gains direction and order; yet confusion provides the energy for focus. As the qualities of both begin to mingle, a solution emerges, bringing with it a feeling we call "clarity."

Clarity implies clear vision that includes all aspects, both good and bad. With clarity, we can see our mistakes as well as our accomplishments. Both have their values, for with each we gain a different insight. We can see what in the past has worked and what has not, and from an objective viewpoint we can question the values we hold. Clarity, then, is the integrated quality of the polar opposites, and as such constitutes the core of confusion. Without first undergoing confusion, we would gain no clarification.

Once more, the performer behind the block of stagefright cannot see this relationship and, in an attempt to avoid confusion, conjectures that the only way to combat this inner state is by forcefully controlling his or her thoughts. For the performer, the answer to confusion seems to be in strict mental concentration, and that is the quality he or she projects to the other side (figure 6.3).

Again we have a setup between mutated opposites—here between confusion and concentration—the same situation as that between the Doubter and the Dogmatist.

Confusion, like fear and anger, looms largest just before performance time, when thoughts are swirling and a memory blank seems imminent. However, rather than trying to harness the mind with excessive reminders, we more often than not can calm the mind another way—by simply living in our confusion for a few minutes just to observe the sensations it creates in the body. This provides a point of focus for the mind, and by that a channel is opened through which it can work.

Some performers have gone a step further with the idea of

Figure 6.3.   Confusion Matrix

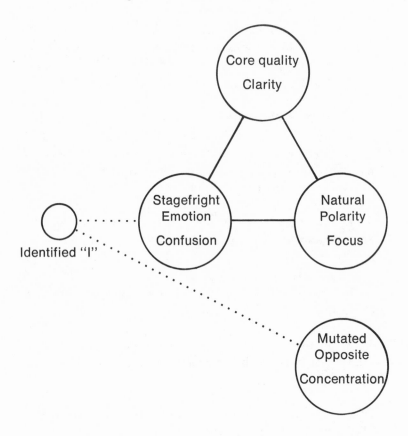

living in their confusion. For example, on several occasions in workshops performers have attempted to exaggerate their confusion. One way they have done this is by *trying* to draw a memory blank when performing before the group. But when they *tried* to forget, they simply could not do so. When they lived in their confusion, they remembered their lines. In our language, their confusion found focus, and together these produced a point of clarity.

Most of us, of course, try a different approach. We try to *think* away the confusion we *feel*, assuming that our thoughts can control our feelings. Admittedly this is true, to a point, since thoughts influence feelings; thus we must think about what we feel. But we must also *feel* what we feel, for if we do not, we are likely to come up with presupposed judgments about our emotions—judgments that are usually wrong and that intensify our stagefright.

The Emotional Power Source

Experiencing our energy is the key to transforming stagefright. In all the accounts given thus far, nothing happened until the person involved lived for a while in his or her emotions. The feelings hold the energy. More accurately, emotion *is* the energy; and although thoughts influence emotions, the transformation per se occurs in the energy itself. Only when the feelings are experienced, validated, and acknowledged do the energies discharge, and with this discharge they find the same frequency as their polar opposite. Once that happens, the two opposites begin to fuse and thus reveal the core essence they hold.

As already stressed, the core qualities of stagefright cannot be presupposed. We cannot enter into confusion, for example, and expect that a sense of clarity will be the outcome. Presupposition cuts us off from the organic resolution of our emotions and causes the stagefright emotions to seek mutant polarities. With confusion, we describe its mutant opposite as the desire for strict concentration; with anger, we call its mutant opposite, rigid control; and for the mutant of fear, we speak of blind confidence. All are the wrong answers for stagefright.

The real answer appears when we suspend our presuppositions and enter the feelings innocently—without expectation. Then the natural polar opposites begin to stir—confusion calls forth focus, anger beckons tranquility, and fear activates courage. As the opposites fuse, the core emotion begins to emerge.

The energy of stagefright becomes utterly transformed. Confusion reveals clarity, anger embraces compassion, and fear bursts into joy. These qualities are at the heart of stagefright; they are not unattainable pipe dreams, but reality. By our choosing to experience the feelings of stagefright, we become the active agent. We select them, not the other way around. As a result, stagefright loses its peculiar power over us. Our act of choice allows the energy of stagefright to transform itself.

Throughout this chapter, we have seen that performers under the influence of the mutated states avoid their feelings. In fact, the three states we have discussed in this connection—control, concentration, and blind confidence—are covers for our true feelings. The concepts of these mutated states are so wrought into us by our training that we pursue these qualities automatically. This means we discount our feelings, we intellectualize about our emotions, we project our feelings onto others and do so without knowing it. And as we do, we increase the feelings of stagefright; for by dodging our feelings, we intensify the emotions we hope to avoid.

CHAPTER 7

Masking Feelings

MOST PERSONS IN THIS COUNTRY are uneasy about showing feelings of any sort. Men, especially, are schooled to think that to express emotion is somehow wrong, and that displaying sensitivity shows weakness. Showing sensitivity, of course, is not nearly so much a problem for women. Nevertheless, whether male or female, we are reluctant to show our stagefright, for we have the idea that acknowledging its presence will cause its energy to turn more fierce. In short, performers fear their fright will grow. Rather than risk losing control, we attempt to mask our stagefright in the hope of controlling it. Admittedly, the feelings of stagefright do flare up upon acknowledgment, but only initially. More important, acknowledging the feelings allows them to transform, while masking them causes a greater threat.

RATIONALIZATIONS

Rationalizing is an attempt to intellectualize our emotions. We talk and think about the problem of stagefright rather than experience it. In other words, we use the conceptual part of our minds to remedy a problem that concerns the feeling part of our soul. Without experiencing the feelings, we make presuppositions about them. We *think* we know what to do for stagefright (we need to control it, think positively, etc.) before we have the experience of it. We thus avoid validating its feeling. Thinking and talking about stagefright "freezes" the action, so to speak. We try to cram the experience of feelings into a preconceived analysis.

If we decide the remedy for stagefright is to conquer our feelings, we are drawing on a mutated polarity. All the mistaken answers discussed in the last chapter—blind confidence, rigid concentration, and total control—are based on the denial of the stagefright emotions, and all are rationalizations. The solution lies in finding a way to experience the feeling and *then* to think about the encounter. The intellect does not work alone in solving the problem of stagefright, but has an equal partner in the emotions.

The fault in rationalization lies in the disproportionate use of the thinking process, whereby the feelings are discounted. To deny emotions paradoxically intensifies their force, and this is what happens with rationalization. Emotions are suppressed and feelings turn into desires. Caring changes to craving, hope shifts to longing, and contentment yields to despair. We scorn whatever emotions we hold and desire other feelings we *think* we ought to possess. So, on the other side of the coin, we can say that rationalizations stem also from emotions, from the desires of dissatisfaction. Desire and rationalization, then, play off each other in a double feedback system. One gives rise to the other, and with both we discount the feelings of stagefright.

DESIRES

Desires are different from genuine needs. Needs have to do with primary necessities for sustenance and natural growth. The basic emotional needs for performers are few in number, although vital in effect. A sense of commitment, purpose, compassion, and encouragement are all basic necessities, and we need not only possess these qualities, but also to share them with others. Above these, however, is the need for fulfillment. No matter what our performing job may be, we need to gain from it a certain life-giving enrichment. If any of these basic requirements is neglected, our need turns to desire—the natural impulse to satisfy our need mutates into a lust to gratify our desires. Desires often masquerade as needs, but they are not vital for performance growth. In fact, they may prove detrimental. All the mutated polarities we have discussed represent the *desires* of the various stagefright subpersonalities—the Critic desires the absolute standards set by the Perfectionist, the Doubter craves the unquestioning certainty promulgated by the Dogmatist, and the Weakling yearns for the particular brand of confidence assured by the Protector. These desires spring up because the real needs of the Critic, the Doubter, and the Weakling are not being met.

By far the most frequent desire of the performer identified with these subpersonalities is the hunger for success, a desire tied most directly to the Perfectionist, although linked to all three mutated opposites. The desire for success bubbles up when the need for enrichment is neglected, and sometimes the two terms, success and enrichment, are confused. Enrichment, though, does not depend upon success and success does not necessarily constitute enrichment. The motives behind the two are in many ways incongruous. The purpose behind enrichment is philanthropic in nature, whereas the purpose behind success is self-indulgent. In short, one is a basic need; the other, a burning desire.

Although the desire for success assumes many forms, its two most common modes of expression are the desire to impress others and the drive to acquire money. Either of these may surpass in importance the quality of our performance; and when that happens, we have a sure sign that real needs are not being met. If any of us craves advancement at the expense of others, somewhere we are lacking satisfaction of a basic need. The truth however is this: if an individual finds a way to satisfy a *basic* need, he or she will likewise find a way toward true advancement; but if that person follows a craving for success at any cost, somewhere along the way he or she will pay a heavy price. Desires, like rationalizations, lead to a dead end.

As we said, desires and rationalizations are interrelated. Both lead to the same wrong answers and both deny present emotions, but they differ in one respect. Although desires are based on denying presently felt emotions, they are themselves an emotion—of yearning, of longing for something else—whereas rationalizations are based on intellect, at least superficially. Nevertheless, desires seek to mask, even conquer, feelings. If, for example, we feel the uncertainty of fear, we desire to rid ourselves of apprehension and cloak ourselves instead with unflinching confidence. The confidence we seek, out of our desire to conquer fear, is a kind of pseudocertainty, in which we are coolly controlled and unaffected by any feelings. We called it blind confidence. Because blind confidence represents a feigned condition, it is not a natural emotion in the true sense, but the rationalization of an emotion. Through desires we seek to snuff out stagefright and to substitute an intellectualized state. In snuffing it out, however, we in effect create deeper feelings, because desires feed on each other. Satisfying one desire raises another.

Let's suppose you have a desire to perform extremely well, but this desire originates from a craving for self-styled glory. If you place every drop of energy on meeting this demand, you first increase the threat of failure; but if you succeed in satisfying this demand, you increase the desire for higher glory. This was the pattern followed by the National Cyclones' football coach. He craved to win, but each time he did, he brought on himself a new hunger. His reasoning or, better, his rationalization, went something like this: "Okay. Last week we beat the Western Reds, but this week we've got to trounce the Eastern Blues, or we'll lose face" (meaning, *I'll* lose face).

Like many performers he confused purpose and enrichment with success. Worse yet, his idea of success was based on the concept bigger is better. For him, the bigger the wins and the higher the score, the better the coach—or so he thought. His desires caused him to follow a pattern of action we called the Pessimistic Victor script.

Scripts and rationalizations are practically synonymous. Both are protective devices to discount feelings, yet both lead to stronger desires on the one hand and greater uncertainties on the other.

The challenge for all of us in dealing with desires is that we give up our longings and preconceived expectations. If we preconceive nothing, nothing need be feared. We need not, however, relinquish vision and purpose. We can give up preconceptions without losing a sense of commitment. If we suspend these preconceptions, we leave ourselves open to discovery, even amazement. We can care without craving, guide without enslaving, and most of all, we can be content without being complacent. By accepting whatever exists in the moment, we can guide our actions with commitment and care. In this way our growth as performers will be unencumbered by discontent and yearning for rewards. With satisfaction and accomplishment we will expand our horizons naturally, for that is our innate purpose—to improve and perfect ourselves. And we will do so from a well-grounded base.

Desires and rationalizations hide this base. They are covers for a dissatisfaction and justification; the one a twisted manifestation of feelings, the other a superficial process of thought. Intellect and emotion in this circumstance remain split, neither being fulfilled. Because they fail to find expression, they discharge themselves onto others as projections.

PROJECTIONS

To understand how projections are made, we can call to mind the principle behind the Rorschach test, in which an abstract pattern or inkblot is shown to an individual who is asked what he or she perceives. From the inkblot one can see almost anything—clouds, meadows, dragons, friends, enemies, pets. Whatever is seen is called a projection, in which some quality, perception, characteristic, or personality trait of the viewer is "projected" onto the abstract pattern. Everyone, in fact, projects. We superimpose the feelings within us onto something outside ourselves. Not only do we do this with inkblots, we do it with other persons. We project our qualities onto them and view their traits from our personal vantage point. In fact, all our observations are based on our own viewpoint, since it is impossible to get inside another's head and experience his or her modus operandi firsthand. Because we cannot achieve direct experience of another's feelings, we are able to perceive in them only those qualities which we, ourselves, possess. This means that the traits we spot in others are part of our own personality, else they would remain unknown to us. We cannot see what we do not possess.

The term *projection*, however, has a more specific connotation. Projections usually refer to those qualities in ourselves of which we are unaware, but which we attribute to others—traits both admirable as well as annoying. Those who marvel at another's ability for organization may find later on that they have the same quality they admired. On the other hand, persons who constantly complain of others' criticisms may discover that they are the ones, in reality, who are critical of them. Both situations are activated by traits in the projector's personality. The first trait may be found to be acceptable, the second, unacceptable. But the individual is unaware of possessing either.

Like desires and rationalizations, projections stem from a denial of feelings. What we reject in ourselves, we project onto others, and the contents of our projections hold our rationalizations and desires. Since projections arise from suppressed emotions, it is difficult to see what feelings are being neglected unless we look at the thought patterns that are generated—those carried by the subpersonalities with which we may be unconsciously identified.

All subpersonalities have a world view and see situations through different colored glasses. Figuratively, we can say that subpersonalities in the stagefright cluster wear dark glasses, while those on "the other side" wear clearer lenses. When we are identified with certain subpersonalities, our view of the world is influenced by the color of their lenses. Although we can project the colors of any subpersonality onto others, those subpersonalities that cause the biggest problems as far as stagefright is concerned are the Critic, the Doubter, and the Protector.

Suppose you are to give a performance soon and, unknowingly, you are identified with an inner Critic who sees the world angrily—through blood red glasses. With you thus influenced, every word or action of others will seem tinged with scarlet. Even warm compliments can be turned into prickly heat.

"My teacher says she cares, but she's such a perfectionist, she'll choke with every mistake I make."

"My boss patted me on the back, but that means 'close the deal, or else.' "

Such reactions are quite similar to compliment discounts, except here the compliment is not only discounted, it is distorted into an accusation. In this case all the important information comes after the "but"—"But she's such a perfectionist," "But that means 'close the deal, or else.' " In addition to the projected accusation, both examples allude to demands for higher expectations, and the two attitudes—accusation and expectation—often go together, reflecting the viewpoint of the Critic. Still, they are projections of the speaker.

One's attitude toward superiors is especially influenced by

Critic projections. If an individual thinks, "My boss watches me like a hawk," it could be that this person, himself, is the one who draws the beady eye on the boss, waiting to catch his first mistake. Or, if the person thinks, "That co-worker of mine is so narrow-minded he never listens to anyone" (meaning, he never listens to me), it could imply that the speaker is the one who is narrow-minded and never listens. As projections, both statements serve to cover inwardly directed anger, since this is the feeling carried by the Critic.

- With Doubter projections, we imagine that others constantly question our abilities.
- "My boss doesn't think I'm ready to take on the prestigious Harding account, so why even bother to ask about it?"
- "The coach says I'm really good, but he's just saying that to bolster my ego, because he's not sure I can win the game."

Not only does this last speaker doubt the coach, he feels the coach doubts him. On top of that, he doubts himself. More specifically, he doubts his ability to measure up to the demands of his inner Critic and therefore projects this self-doubt onto the coach. The feeling he masks from himself is one of uncertainty and confusion.

Projections of the Protector are easy to spot in others but illusive to detect in ourselves. Again, the Protector's function is to protect the Weakling against fear—at least, this is his purpose on the surface. His real intent is to keep the Weakling feeling victimized. Consequently, an individual making Protector projections assumes everyone is out to get him.

- "My closest rival wished me good luck, but I know she's just waiting for me to fall on my face."
- "The audience is just sitting there like a pack of wolves, waiting for me to make the first mistake."

In either of these cases, the individual sees others more or less as frauds. In the second example the audience apparently comes not to enjoy a performance, but to condemn it. In pointing this out, the speaker appears to be a virtuous victim, at the mercy of all. However, he is hardly virtuous, since it is he who chops down others, in this case by calling them wolves. In times past he has likely been a wolf in the audience, or why else would he assume that others might respond in kind to him?

It is true that sometimes other persons actually *are* out to "get" us. No doubt about it, they do indeed question our abilities and criticize our efforts. If this is truly the case, then our point of view is not projection (in the specific sense), but simple observation. In such instances, others are probably projecting their stagefright onto us, and we have two options in meeting such a situation. We can decide either to assert ourselves against the threats of such malevolent persons, or we can view them objectively as puppets of their own subpersonalities. If we are not puppets of our own inner voices, their behavior will affect us less strongly. In fact, it will have little effect, unless we are identified with the same subpersonalities as they.

For example, let's say that on a particular occasion you are in a happy-go-lucky mood, and a friend approaches with a scowl on his face. Quite likely, you will dismiss the furrowed brow with, "Gee, it looks like old Jim got up on the wrong side of the bed this morning." The situation changes dramatically, however, if you, yourself, are in an ill temper. His frown becomes yours, because you are identified with the same subpersonality, and in time you both will probably begin to project your Critics onto each other.

Any time we feel powerless in a given situation, we need to give attention to the question of projection, and for two reasons. First, projections are our responsibility. We are in a much better position to change our projections than we are to remold others' viewpoints. Yet, surprisingly, when we give up projections, others' attitudes toward us seem to change. Second, projections, so far as performers are concerned, are usually cast primarily on close professional associates, and we may think we are powerless in a given situation, when, in fact, we are not.

The problem begins when professional associates form part

of our audience. The audience may comprise any number, from one to thousands, and projections may be made to any whom we consider significant observers. These can include all kinds of authority figures, friends, or, perhaps even more importantly, competitors. We *think* the audience is critical, doubting, or malicious toward us (depending on the subpersonality being projected), when in actuality this is not true.

Not long ago, a player in a symphony orchestra told of the pressure she felt on one particular occasion while watching the audience just before a concert. She gazed into the hall and spotted two persons laughing and talking. She could feel her resentment growing as she thought to herself, "How silly they are now, but in a moment they'll be judging me, and they are totally unqualified for that."

This was obviously a case of projection. How could she know the qualifications of two strangers, or, in fact, that they would be judging her in a moment? Still, such a projection is typical of performers, and the attitude most frequently projected is that of the Critic, as was the case here.

At times, some projections to the audience can be transmitted more strongly than others. We perceive that one audience is more difficult to perform for than another. Generally speaking, performers conclude that knowledgeable audiences are more critical than naive ones. A newspaper reporter, for example, may experience acute stagefright when speaking to a specialized few at a press convention, yet have no problem delivering a general talk to a gathering of the local garden club. The problem can work the other way, too. A highly trained specialist, such as a scientist, might shudder at the prospect of explaining complicated material to an inexperienced audience. He or she may outwardly project that the audience is too dumb to understand complicated issues, but the Critic may be saying inwardly that *he* or *she* is too dumb to explain things simply.

Some performers find it more difficult to perform in front of friends than before a sea of strangers, again mainly because of

Critic projections. Even though friends may provide support and comfort, the performer may worry about the prospect of letting them down by performing poorly. In effect, that person imagines they hold high expectations for the performance. Unless this individual has false friends, though, such an attitude shows a Critic projection, in which the performer's own high expectation is attributed to others. True friends are not let down by a weak performance. Generally, they hold only one expectation for their performing acquaintances: that the performer do his or her best. In addition, they realize that few performers intentionally give anything less than their best—a point sometimes discounted by the person on stage, but one all of us might remember. Rarely do performers deliberately put forth their second-best effort. Nobody gives a deficient performance on purpose.

Audiences, in general, appreciate this same point; they assume that the performers in any given circumstance try their best. For the most part, audiences root for performers, even the losing team. They do not expect impossible feats, nor do they revel when a performer falls on his face. If they do, that is their concern, not ours. Such an attitude on their part shows what subpersonalities govern their lives, not ours. This does not mean that audiences cannot be highly critical. We can profit from their criticism, if we weigh the validity of their remarks, rather than view them as a personal affront. With reference to the subject at hand, though, if we feel an audience is against us, we must first ask ourselves whether we are projecting. We may find a surprise in store, as in the two following examples.

John, a clarinet student, came for a private session and reported that he could play very well under any circumstance, unless he knew his teacher would be listening. I asked him if he would carry on an imaginary dialogue with his teacher to see what lay behind this inconsistency. As the conversation unfolded, John let it be known that he wanted more compliments from his teacher. He felt that the teacher withheld compliments and demanded impossible goals in order to keep him working. But when he changed roles and became the teacher, he discovered the teacher wanted more communication from John, in order to help him play more beautifully.

I intervened here and asked the "teacher" if he would demonstrate right now to "John" what beautiful playing sounded like. And indeed he did. The "teacher" played two exquisite phrases of music. Smiling, I reacted, "Now tell John what he needs to do to play as beautifully as that."

"Well, he needs to free up his body, come out from behind the music stand, relax his lips a bit more, and, most of all, show some enthusiasm for what he is doing."

The session continued with the "teacher" giving "John" valuable suggestions about performing with excellence, and "John" responding with enthusiasm. Each gave to the other.

It was an exciting session in which the real John learned he had been projecting his own Critic onto his teacher, a practice that was the main source of his stagefright. He also found that his Critic at the core had some wise suggestions about performance. The Critic became his own inner mentor, and John's attitude changed from one of defensive hesitancy to that of assurance, backed by inner knowledge and strength.

Another student discovered a different aspect of projections. In the past, he had projected his Critic onto another classmate. Every time he made a mistake, he found himself wondering what the friend might be thinking. On realizing what he had been doing, he changed his attitude toward the friend, and found, surprisingly, that the friend's censorship of him (and of others) mellowed considerably. The interesting question is this: Who did the mellowing? The critical friend or the student who had made the projection? Amazingly, whatever we give out, we get back in return. If we project our Critic onto others, theirs will likely be projected onto us, and our stagefright will probably grow.

Although both the foregoing accounts show how performers project traits onto particular individuals, such projections represent habitual patterns of the way in which one views the audience. Usually it matters little who is in the audience. If an individual is inclined to make projections, he or she will find someone on whom to cast an attitude regardless. Later in the session with John, for example, it dawned on him that even when his teacher was not in the audience, he tended to transfer his projection to another authority figure. The same realization also surfaced later in the second account. The student discovered there *always* seemed to be a friend in the audience. Even before he knew the friend in question, he had had previous confidants, and every time he had made a mistake, he wondered what they might be thinking.

We may ascribe our stagefright to a particular individual, but the truth is we often look for another person to blame for our own internal turmoil. The old saying, There's one in every crowd, takes on new meaning in light of projections. If we find a critic in every audience, it could well be of our own making. An audience is an audience, and we can turn it into a friend or foe by the projections we make.

MUTATED PROJECTIONS

As the term suggests, mutated projections are our projections of the mutated subpersonalities. Traits of the Perfectionist, Dogmatist, and Protector are attributed to others—traits which seem admirable, but in reality originate from the stagefright cluster.

Take the Protector, for example. Remember that the Protector has two sides. His hidden side (and his true nature) casts a shadow of deceit, but his outer surface (and his false front) shines with deceptive brilliance. He is the one with the magic power that promises to turn frogs to princes, but who in reality casts a curse. Mutated projections, however, show only his outward appearance—his bright coat of protection. In fact, mutated projections show only the superficial positive aspects of any of the mutated subpersonalities.

When individuals project these mutated qualities, other persons seem to present absolute models of excellence (the Perfectionist), possess all the correct answers (the Dogmatist), or hold almost magical powers (the Protector). They seem to be supremely talented, confident, disciplined, organized, and the like. In short, those who are influenced by mutated projections tend to be hero worshippers. They see enviable qualities in others and wish the same for themselves.

Mutated projections are in fact projected desires. As such, they give the same wrong information we have heard before. In other words, we seek cocksure confidence, rigid concentration, and total control, and ascribe these characteristics to others. This is a mistake. First of all, others probably do not have these qualities (at least not to the degree of our projection), and, more important, these qualities are the wrong answers for stagefright. We will never find this out, however, as long as we continue to aim these mutated projections at others, because projections—mutated or not—arise from masked feelings. And the thicker the mask, the stronger the feelings.

We can gain valuable information from our projections, however, by examining our perceptions of others. Every time we suffer stagefright in the presence of another individual, we can observe his or her most characteristic quality, whether admired or disliked, and ask ourselves these questions: Is there any way the trait I see in this person could be part of me? Is the trait I see one I dislike, admire, or crave to possess? What would my performance be like if I expressed in it the same quality I perceive?

The point of asking and answering these questions is to own our projections, because in doing so we can better direct the energy they waste. When we own our projections, they dissolve into simple observations about others and lose their influential power. Owning projections also can reveal startling discoveries about the qualities we possess. John, the clarinetist, discovered that his projected teacher revealed an inner mentor. The student who worried about his friend's reactions, discovered inside himself a mellow companion. The qualities we see in others dwell as well in us; the projections arise when we discount what lives within.

Projections share the same basis as rationalizations and desires. All are different aspects of the same issue—the masking of feelings. But the answer for stagefright is found by unmasking the feelings we reject, because in that experience the energy of stagefright begins to change. As their core essence is revealed, our feelings transform and our thought patterns assume a new viewpoint. When this happens, we begin to move through the block of stagefright. When we do, we meet new subpersonalities—those that create the voices from the other side.

CHAPTER 8

Voices from
the Other Side

REMEMBERING THE DISCUSSION in which we found that anger working in conjunction with its natural polarity ultimately evolves into compassion, that fear turns to joy, and confusion to clarity, we can begin to see how the corresponding subpersonalities—the angry Critic, the fearful Weakling, and the confused Doubter—all flower into higher, more evolved personages.

In considering which personages evolve, however, we need to keep in mind that we speak of generalized prototypes and not absolute, predictable patterns. As already stressed, no one can guarantee which qualities emerge from the other side, and, therefore, we do not attest that the voices from the other side of stagefright will unfold in the precise way described in this chapter. With each individual, the transaction is unique. Thus, in explaining the process we shall describe not what *will* happen, but what *can* happen—and what *has* happened to others in the past.

THE CRITIC TRANSFORMATION

When we first considered the basic issues of stagefright, we called the Critic's polar opposite the Commender, because commendation is the natural polar opposite of criticism. When the energy of the Critic is validated, he connects with the Commender. With reference to the Critic's energy, we saw that the feeling of anger holds tranquility as its natural polarity. Thus, we can now associate tranquility with the Commender and see more clearly the diametrical position the Commender holds vis-a-vis the Critic. As the name suggests, the Commender is the subpersonality that offers inner encouragement. The Commender is the one that notices the valuable aspects of our performing efforts and, despite our shortcomings, points out the unique contributions we have to offer. Hearing the angry judgments of the Critic, the Commender responds with composure, giving encouragement. One reacts with contempt; the other answers with quiet esteem.

Perhaps the most pointed message of the Commender came to Joe, the musician who first visualized his stagefright as a bat. Although Joe passed through several stages, the turning point in his session came after his decision to experience his angry Critic, who appeared in the form of a scary animal. When he puffed himself up, playing the angry beast, his Critic changed. It gave Joe an honest appraisal of what he feared most: "He's afraid he will find out he is not as good as he ought to be."

Following this remark, Joe made his first contact with the other side, when with quiet conviction he said, "I know deep down that how I play does not affect my total worth as a person." This was the Commender speaking, and it was activated by Joe's willingness to express his Critic honestly.

From this account we get a hint that, despite their opposition, the Critic and Commender (as is the general case with natural polarities) are occupied with the same issues. Both seek a performance of quality (this was the issue behind Joe's pointed remarks) and both speak with active concern, even though their voices carry a different tone. Most of all, they share an evaluative quality, and this is what binds them together. It is also the quality that can keep them apart, if the evaluative sense of the Commender is replaced by the judgmental advice of his mutated counterpart, the Perfectionist.

Although the Commender shares the Perfectionist's concern for competence, the level the Commender hopes to achieve is attainable. Further, the Commender builds on attributes we possess. The Perfectionist *discounts* what we have, commanding that we pursue something we can never accomplish—unattainable perfectionism. With this attitude of gripping control, he restrains our development, but the Commender fosters our growth by responding with quiet enthusiasm.

The biggest difference between these two lies in the fact that the Commender listens to the Critic. In order for commendation to gain credence, it must be subject to criticism; and conversely, for criticism to bear fruit, it must include commendation. Both the Critic and the Commender weigh our actions, and as their evaluative purpose falls into alignment, their energy begins to mingle. Anger and tranquility play off each other, finding fusion in compassion. With that, a new subpersonality, one of a higher order, springs forth to express that quality.

Thus we meet the first of a trio of subpersonalities that not only combine the qualities of the natural polarities, but also reveal the core essences inbred in the stagefright subpersonalities. Since the first member of this group combines the Critic's power and the Commender's tranquility, we can designate him the Mentor, for he is a loyal advisor.

Not only does the Mentor have compassion, he holds the ability to make sound judgments. Like the subpersonalities from which he springs, the Mentor is an evaluator, but more than that he is a discriminator, a "person" of vision whose perception is based on experience. Through him is strengthened our power of discernment, and this discernment carries with it a mixture of empathy and evaluation. In short, he is our inner "friend" and he receives us with the warmth of affection.

But this affection is by no means pallid. Compassion, as we have explained before, is not the same as sympathy. Sympathy conveys the suggestion of helplessness and pity, but compassion carries strength, because it is filled with enthusiastic involvement. The Mentor, as a consequence, possesses potency; though his attitude is commending, it is likewise commanding, because he cares about the way in which we perform.

In helping us perform to the best of our ability, the Mentor has at hand several tactics that serve as a guide for improvement. Sometimes he is pragmatic, offering timely advice about rectifying certain problems. He may, for example, give useful suggestions about preparation: "You need to outline your facts," or, "This passage needs more work." In this function he reveals his quietly discerning side—caring, but never condemning. On the other hand, he may take a lighthearted approach in his suggestions. Such was the tactic shown John, the clarinetist, who engaged his "teacher" in dialogue. The Teacher-Mentor encouraged John to move out from behind the music stand and show enthusiasm for what he was doing—to have a little fun in performing.

So, we can say that the voice of the Mentor carries several tones—sometimes profound, sometimes pragmatic. In any case, it conveys an attitude of support. Combining the energy of anger, the preserve of tranquility, and the care of compassion, the Mentor fashions a message of integrity. From the Mentor we gain the power to make honest evaluations.

Still, let us remember that contact with our inner friend is made through the Critic, who is part of the integrated quality. A kernel of the Mentor lives in the Critic, as well as in the Commender. But the movement toward integration begins with the Critic, since the performer is identified (initially) with him. Thus, through our validation of his energy, the Critic is transformed; his core quality of honest discernment is revealed. And this core is what guides our growth as performers (figure 8.1).

Figure 8.1. The Critic Transformation

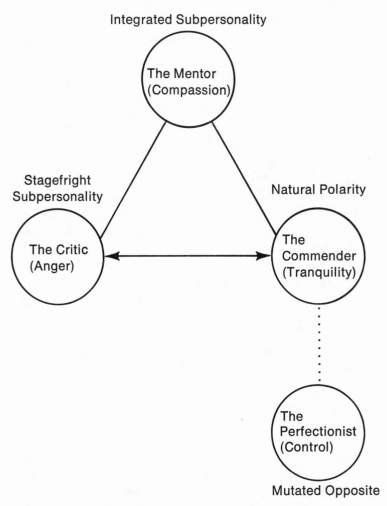

Integrated Subpersonality

The Mentor
(Compassion)

Stagefright
Subpersonality

Natural Polarity

The Critic
(Anger)

The
Commender
(Tranquility)

The
Perfectionist
(Control)

Mutated Opposite

Author's note: In this and subsequent diagrams in this chapter, the mutated opposite is included to show its proximity (diagrammatically) to the natural polarity with which it is falsely associated (indicated by the dotted line).

THE WEAKLING TRANSFORMATION

A different kind of growth evolves from the next subpersonality in the stagefright cluster. What we just described regarding the Critic's transformation might be termed a nurturing kind of growth. What we are about to consider could be called a growth from adventure.

Fear, as we already know, is the feeling held by the Weakling, and the natural polarity of that emotion we saw to be courage. Since fear plays off courage, so do the subpersonalities associated with these two energies—the Weakling and the Risker. They are reciprocal in nature. Without weakness there is nothing to risk, and without risk there is no perception of weakness. Moreover, each subpersonality contributes a certain quality to our actions. In facing risk, the Weakling, because of his apprehension, brings not only prudence but a measure of sensitivity, while the Risker, because of his valor, contributes an element of thrill and adventure. Their energies of fear and courage interweave, producing joy. And since the joy is a product of exploration, we can call the subpersonality who represents this integration, the Discoverer (figure 8.2).

Propelled by the excitement of joy, the Discoverer strikes out on new paths by which we can approach our craft. Under his influence we encounter both success and failure, and from each we can glean valuable information important to our growth. Giving us new ideas with which to experiment, the Discoverer offers us refreshment and vitality, because through him our performance is rejuvenated.

The findings of the Discoverer need not be monumental to be meaningful. Sometimes the most useful discoveries we make are small ones—a slight change in body posture, maybe a different way in which to look at the audience. Actually, some of our discoveries may be temporary, discarded, or perhaps modified with the disclosure of other findings. In fact, rarely do we find

Figure 8.2. The Weakling Transformation

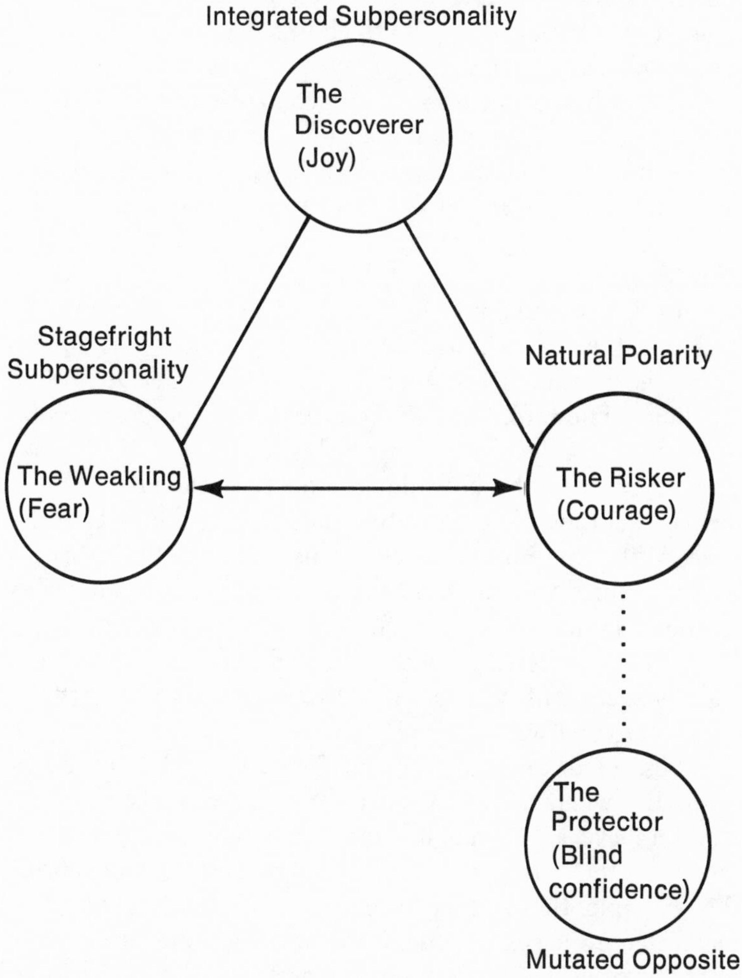

Integrated Subpersonality

The
Discoverer
(Joy)

Stagefright
Subpersonality

Natural Polarity

The Weakling
(Fear)

The Risker
(Courage)

The
Protector
(Blind
confidence)

Mutated Opposite

from the Discoverer a definitive answer that needs no further
probing.

Once in a private session Mike, a basketball player, worked

with guided imagery as a means to examine his fear of shooting free throws. He could shoot baskets easily in the heat of play, when he had little time to think; but when he had free reign, something inside caused him to choke. After working through some of his images of fear, he saw an image of a tank that symbolized for him the courage he needed to offset his choking. He concluded that everytime he felt himself tighten up, he could evoke the image of the tank, sensing its pervasive power. For him this was a meaningful discovery—at least it was that day. Two weeks later he came again and reported that the tank, although helpful for evoking a kind of inner assurance, lacked agility. Then he told how he had found a better solution on his own. First, he thought about the image for a few days. (In our terms he consulted the Mentor to evaluate the Discoverer's finding.) The tank was *too* powerful for his purpose—too aggressive. It caused him to force his shots, sending the ball bounding off the backboard and away from the basket. So, he evoked another image, and this time he got the picture of a tree. With this image he felt strength, especially in his legs which seemed to grow from the floor; but he also felt agility, particularly in his arms, which, like branches, seemed to float upward. By reassessing the tank, he had arrived at a more helpful discovery. His Mentor and Discoverer worked together to find a better answer.

Thus, we discard some of our discoveries, while others we keep. But whatever we do, we find that the insights of the Discoverer have a fundamental consistency—a fact revealed in nearly all the personal accounts, despite their varying content. For example, Beth, who played the guitar with her body alternately tense and spastic, discovered latent flexibility; the woman who "became" the turtle (and later exclaimed, "Wow, I feel so tall") gained a new kinesthetic space; the speaker who spoke from behind the pile of chairs found a closer communication with his audience—in effect, though, all found the same thing. They discovered special power within themselves and a special power that was unique to them. Finding this special power is what is consistent about the Discoverer's insights, and for all of us the issue at base is the same. We keep discovering this unique essence. It is not a power we have never known, but more likely one we have forgotten. With each new experience we discover a different facet of its nature, so that with each time we find it, we seemingly greet it anew. This creates the joy carried by the Discoverer.

There is, however, a related issue in the Discoverer's findings —and that is the close kinship of the energies involved (fear, courage, and joy) and the fact that they all come together in the discovery of our inner power. All the individuals we have cited experienced a sense of vulnerability before they made any significant discoveries. They were afraid, yet by acknowledging their vulnerability they found strength. The Weakling, as we know, is the subpersonality who holds fear and tries to protect his vulnerability. Paradoxically, however, it is precisely his vulnerability that contains strength. Vulnerability houses deep inside itself a basic honesty—a naked truth, if you will, and this truth is the strength. An incredible fullness is ours when we accept the fact of our vulnerability. Because when we do, we live in a moment of truth, a moment in which a mystery is solved, a reality exposed. Then, with this exposure, the grip of stagefright releases its hold.

We can remember the experience of Joe, who, upon unraveling the secret of vulnerability, said, "It seems the more vulnerable I become, the more honest I feel. Yet, as I grow more honest, the feelings of vulnerability subside. The tension seems to release."

With this perception Joe discovered the secret held by the Weakling. When he accepted his vulnerability, he had no need for protection, and thus, having no need for protection, gave himself genuine strength.

Of course, finding our inner strength is a discovery of paramount importance, but we come back to the earlier statement that our discoveries need not be monumental to be meaningful. All are meaningful, for whatever we learn about ourselves—be it major or minor, discarded or kept—reveals a portion of our inner essence. Each discovery is an important stepping-stone to our next level of development. As important as each seems to be at the time, another awaits our discovery, for growth never ceases. But any discovery, no matter its magnitude, needs further consideration. The Discoverer does not work alone. This sensitive adventurer, whether he finds the profound pleasure of performance, or makes lesser discoveries along the way, needs in any case to have an evaluation of his findings. Therefore, he works with the Mentor, who offers counsel about the discoveries. It is not enough to know that we possess a special might; we must also understand its significance for our performance. Thus, in choosing the path to be trod, these two subpersonalities call on a third, who helps mobilize their energy. This subpersonality has its roots in the Doubter.

THE DOUBTER TRANSFORMATION

Although the Doubter's voice is usually heard first, the message from the subpersonality who evolves from him is frequently heard last. In the same process we have described many times, this evolution arises from the play-off between the Doubter and his natural polarity, a subpersonality we labeled the Believer. The Doubter we saw promotes an uncertainty that leads to confusion, and the natural polarity to confusion we called a state of being focused. So now we can link the Believer with this state, a condition described as an easy centering of one's attention. The implication of this linkage is that if one focuses his attention, he believes in his actions; otherwise, centering his attention would be no easy task.

Focus we contrasted with rigid concentration, an action requiring duty-driven effort and prescribed by the Dogmatist. Thus, remembering that mutated qualities are sometimes mistaken for natural polarities, we can likewise distinguish the messages of the Believer from those of his mutated counterpart, the Dogmatist. We already know the Dogmatist's messages convey certain knowledge, and because they do, they seem to offer the correct remedy for stagefright. We know also how the Dogmatist meets the Doubter's habitual questions—he tells the Doubter to think positively and to concentrate on correcting the problem. In contrast, when the Believer responds to the Doubter, his answers are more commodious, ample to the occasion yet sometimes changing according to circumstances. If he is confronted with a string of "what if" questions ("What if I have a memory slip?" "What if I get phlegm in my throat?" "What if I trip?"—and on and on), the Believer may respond with, "Do you truly believe all this is likely to happen?"

In another circumstance, if the Doubter should ask, "What will happen if I fail?" the Believer might suggest, "Think about what will happen if you succeed."

Rarely, if ever, does the Believer speak in absolutes. He cannot predict the outcome and he offers no guarantee for success. He can, however, offer support and encourage us in our pursuits: "I *believe* you are well prepared for the occasion. See if you are willing to enjoy yourself."

Finally, the answers of the Believer always consider the validity of the Doubter. They all convey in essence, "I hear your doubts. Consider the possibility of believing in yourself."

As is the case with all natural polarities, the Doubter and the Believer represent not only exact opposites, but also direct complements. The Doubter seeks answers from the Believer; one asks, the other answers. Yet the Believer does not respond without the Doubter, for no answer comes until a question is asked.

But there is more than that. His answers invite inquiry. In order for them to have credence, they must be tested; they must be exposed to doubt. Belief grows out of disbelief, not dogma. Doubt strengthens belief. From the interplay of their energies— confusion and focus—there evolves a quality we called clarity. It is a clarity born of conviction, conceived not by doctrine, but by faith—faith in what we do. Thus, the subpersonality who emerges as an expression of this quality we can call the Truster, for his is a clarity built on faith (figure 8.3).

In a way, the Truster is a cumulative subpersonality who emerges last, after certain dynamics in the stagefright cluster

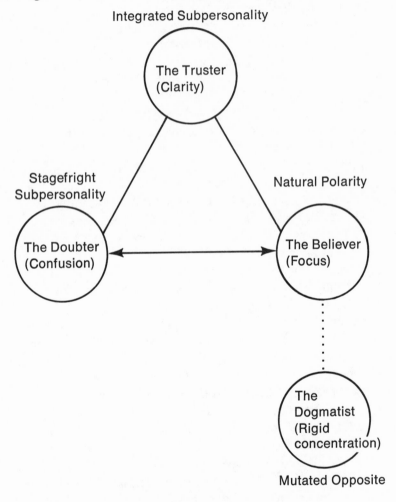

Figure 8.3. The Doubter Transformation

have been validated. Joe was told toward the end of his session to let go of his conscious control and allow the mystery of his music to unfold. Here is the central tone of the Truster's message: have faith in your abilities. Through trust, we mobilize our faculties so that, with singleness of purpose, our total attention is pinpointed on our performance.

The concept of giving up control causes concern for some performers. The dynamics involved need to be clearly defined. Some fear letting go of control will lead to chaos and confusion, but this is true only if we attempt to let go of control when we have never had it. And we gain control by building our skills and polishing our craft with careful preparation. Without that, we cannot let go of control, because we have never possessed it. If we attempt to do so—that is, if we are ill-prepared and simply hope for the best—we will probably fail. Failure is still a possibility, even with thorough preparation—but so is success. The Truster sees both possibilities. After weighing the chances and finding them favorable (with the aid of the Mentor), the Truster invites the performer to have faith in his abilities, to trust his preparation and be content with his level of competency, then to "let go" and allow the performance to unfold.

If we truly accept the possibility that we might fail, we find that we no longer need the confidence to succeed. Indeed, confidence is no longer an issue. That is the irony. Confidence is ours when we no longer need or desire it. With trust comes confidence—not the type of blind confidence we earlier associated with the Protector, or even the determined courage carried by the Risker, but a kind of easy assurance, a comfortable reliance backed by clarity and faith. With trust we become a vessel of the performance—to play as well as to be played upon. The vessel shapes the performance and the performance determines the vessel. Both become indistinguishable: the performer *is* the message, he *is* the music, he *is* the game. Performer and performance are one entity. This is the union that sparks those magic moments we talked about at the beginning of the book,

CARL A. RUDISILL LIBRARY
LENOIR RHYNE COLLEGE

the magic we all hope to find. Such moments are like little glimpses of bliss, where time stands still and we are caught for an instant in eternity.

THE HIGHER SELF

Performers know this higher expression of self with a flash of recognition. Experiencing this phenomenon is an occasion savored by all, for it touches to the quick. Yet in every case it comes as a surprise, when we least expect it.

First, the performer undergoes a period of diligent labor, organizing material and hewing out new ideas about a particular performance concept. The actor searches for the authentic nature of the character; the musician seeks the genuine tone of the piece; the athlete looks for the precise technique needed. After the diligent labor comes a period of despair, a time of frustration when nothing seems to work and all effort seems in vain. The performer sinks back exhausted, expecting the worst. Suddenly, however, everything becomes clear. An actor friend explained it this way: "When nothing I tried caught the spirit of the character, I simply gave up trying, and the character, himself, took over. It was as though a power greater than me provided the energy."

This and similar experiences describe our making contact with a higher essence. It is a juncture brought about by a leap of faith in which we let go of our conscious control and become the performance. In trusting our abilities, we activate a higher essence deep within, but one embedded in the resources of us all.

The energy of this higher essence emanates from a source Roberto Assagioli calls the Higher Self (see figure 3.1). This Higher Self is an observing force and, therefore, not a subpersonality, since it does not participate in direct action. Rather, it is the fountainhead from which creative powers spring. In this way the Higher Self is similar to the Observing "I," but the functions of the two are different. Whereas the Observing "I" is the center of personal identity, concerned with individual personality, the Higher Self incorporates universality as well as individuality.

This more inclusive observer is transpersonal in nature; not only does it observe individual actions, it sees the collective nature of mankind. It is the energy in us all that looks for purpose, understanding, and meaning in our existence. It seeks to perfect itself, not primarily according to the rules of humans, but rather according to the laws of the universe. In short, it is the spiritual seat in all persons and recognized by every religious tradition of the world. In Christian circles, it is called the soul, the in-dwelling of the Holy Spirit. Others, in Eastern religions, refer to the inner Atman, Brahman, Buddha, and others.

Although the concept of the Higher Self is spiritual in nature, we do not have to hold a specific religious belief to accept its power. What we must have, however, is a trust—an acceptance that there dwells somewhere in us a presence wiser than our ordinary workaday awareness. It is a superior understanding that enables us to have direct comprehension of the world about us.

Whenever the Higher Self is revealed to an individual, it often appears in various symbolic images so that the conscious mind can comprehend its meaning. These images represent characteristic aspects of its nature and appear in such forms as a beam of white light, a temple, a flame, a lotus, perhaps a star, or some other emblem of transcendance. Very often, it appears as an ancient sage who holds vast wisdom and whose eyes are full of love and compassion. Many performers who work with guided imagery report seeing such images. After they have worked through their lower subpersonalities, a symbol like one of these emerges, bringing with it an exalted sense of well-being. This is almost always coupled with a supreme insight into matters pertaining to performance.

- "Consider the beauty you communicate."
- "Know who you are."
- "Trust in your purpose."

All these are messages performers have heard from the Higher

Self during guided imagery experiences. Although the messages may resemble in words some of those we have described before, an experience of the Higher Self brings something more. The insights of the Discoverer, the evaluative sense of the Mentor, and the clarified purpose of the Truster come together in a brilliance of truth that flashes in our mind like a star. It is as though we ride the cutting edge of our performance, gliding effortlessly along the way, for we are caught up in the full meaning of our purpose.

It is like a dream. Or so it appears, because the Higher Self exists outside conscious awareness, except for the brief moments when it descends and touches the Observing "I." Its messages instill in us a dream-like inspiration. This inspiration is incomplete without actualization, however, and actualizing the inspiration is *our* duty. Having been filled with the moment, we have the charge to bring the inspiration to fruition. We must understand the meaning of the messages as applied to specific circumstances, then work to ground them by expressing them in explicit actions. Otherwise, the moment of inspiration will vanish like the dream it seems to be.

To be sure, such inspirational moments are elusive. We cannot predict their coming, or force them into coming. Still, there are certain measures we can take to encourage their more frequent appearance. Such measures follow the line of reasoning we have presented all along.

First, we must expand our awareness. As well as we can, we must become acquainted with our lower subpersonalities, particularly those in the stagefright cluster. If we are unacquainted with them, we cannot know their polar opposites on the other side. But if we expand our awareness, we will see the larger whole and perceive how the polar opposites complement each other. As we understand that relationship, we will see the subpersonalities transform themselves into higher entities. In all the diagrams showing integrated feelings and subpersonalities, these entities were placed at the top of a triangle, indicating a movement toward the Higher Self. The final contact, however, is made by the Truster. He is the link to the Higher Self, because trust is the bridge between the known and the unknown.

We remember, though, that trust is based on careful preparation. Therefore, we expend every effort and consider each angle as it relates to performance. After we have done that, however, we can stop and rest, and then give in to faith. This means we give up control and thereby reach the crux of the issue. By letting go of control, we can open ourselves to the energy of the Higher Self. When we are ready—when we are "ripe" to receive its power—it will be revealed. A magic moment will be ours.

If we are not ripe for the moment—if we have not done the necessary groundwork in expanding our awareness—the inspiration we receive may be muddled. Once, for example, a private client using guided imagery saw a beam of white light he associated with his Higher Self. As he looked at the beam, however, it turned into a spotlight, glaring down on a stage. Looking into the source of the light, he saw a vision of an old man who was very wise, he thought. The face, however, was that of his long-respected German teacher—respected, yet held in fear and awe. And the old man gave advice that rang a familiar bell: "You must concentrate harder and acquire greater discipline; then you will perform with confidence." This was not the message of the Higher Self, but of a projected Dogmatist.

The Higher Self is different. It never gives doctrinaire commands or pedantic advice, but rather offers valuable provocation filled with invention. It is concerned with altruistic good and with universal fidelity. This higher reality in ourselves is a feeling, a bodily sensation, a thought pattern—all rolled into one. It reveals a moment of exaltation in which all the elements in the performer's matrix find their ultimate fusion in the Higher Self. This is the climactic voice from the other side of stagefright. When it speaks, all our faculties come together, functioning in a cohesion of purpose and intent. With it, we become a willing instrument for our performance.

CHAPTER 9

The Integral Design

ACHIEVING THE FUSION OF FORCES as revealed by the Higher Self is the goal toward which all of us are directed. And it is a fusion that takes place simultaneously on several fronts: the merging of polar opposites, the syncronization of our bodies, minds, and emotions, the unification of performer and performance, and the synthesis of all the elements in the performer's matrix—the subpersonalities, the Observing "I," and the Higher Self. Thus, the Higher Self represents a coming together of diverse elements to comprise an integral design in which all elements function harmoniously.

In describing this fusion of elements, we have often used the term *integration*. Fusion, unity, synchronism, and all other similar descriptions are also qualities of integration, to be sure, and these we perceive from the viewpoint of the Higher Self. But there is one more step for us to take in order to comprehend the full measure of this higher viewpoint—and that is to see not only the qualities of unity but also those of diversity, to appreciate not just the properties of concord but to understand the attributes of disparity. That is the final step in our grasping the full significance of the Higher Self. It is a step beyond integration.

When the performer passes through the block of stagefright, he or she is stationed at the focal point of the performer's matrix (see figure 3.4). When that happens, all the components of the matrix converge. The Higher Self descends, and the subpersonalities come together at the point of the Observing "I." Hence, the performer at this focal point sees three simultaneous forces at work: disparity, unity, and integration. Put another way, he or she has the viewpoint of the three components—the subpersonalities, the Observing "I," and the Higher Self—thus gaining three levels of perception.

The first level is the perception of disparity and it is revealed by the subpersonalities. On this level the performer sees the elements of stagefright as different from those on the other side. In capsule these differences can be listed this way:

> angry criticism—tranquil commendation
> confused doubt—focused belief
> fearful weakness—courageous risking

One group opposes the other. The collective quality of the group on the left we know to be stagefright, but we have spoken little of the *collective* quality of their natural polarities. Now that we see them in summary form, we can gather that they represent the quality of self-assurance. Thus, stagefright and self-assurance form a natural polarity, and in that their elements are contradictory. Nevertheless, based on what we know, they form a unity in their intent. Both arise from our commitment to purpose. Commitment is their common energy, for without that, neither (in fact, nothing we have discussed) would exist. This is the second level of perception, and it is experienced by the Observing "I," which sees not only the unity of the elements, but also their disparity.

So the performer at the focal point sees both dimensions—stagefright and self-assurance are different from one another in content, yet the same in intent. They are like two suns shining into each other—suns that comprise different elements but nevertheless radiate the same energy into each other. But where does this energy come from?

Again, based on what we know, purpose and commitment come from the Higher Self. Thus, the Higher Self fashions from this unified disparity a new order of reality. And the performer at the centered position sees a third level of perception. It is the integration of stagefright and self-assurance. The differences just listed are combined, transforming themselves into qualities greater than the dichotomous elements. The resulting qualities we can likewise list in capsule form:

compassionate discernment
clarified trust
joyful discovery

Collectively, these qualities lead to a higher expression of self which, when manifested, create in us the essence of fulfillment. Fulfillment thus stands at the top of the integral design. It emanates from the polarity of stagefright and self-assurance (see figure 9.1).

The three levels of perception are the subpersonalities, the Observing "I," and the Higher Self.

At base, what this means is that on one level (that of the subpersonalities), we see stagefright as something disruptive to our equilibrium, and self-assurance as something restorative to our sense of well-being. But on a second level (that of the Observing "I"), we see that in many ways stagefright and self-assurance are the same thing. They are two sides of the same coin. Both emanate from the energy of commitment, and without commitment, performance would be meaningless. But more than that, on a third level (that of the Higher Self), we see that stagefright and self-assurance combine to form a higher

Figure 9.1. The Integral Design

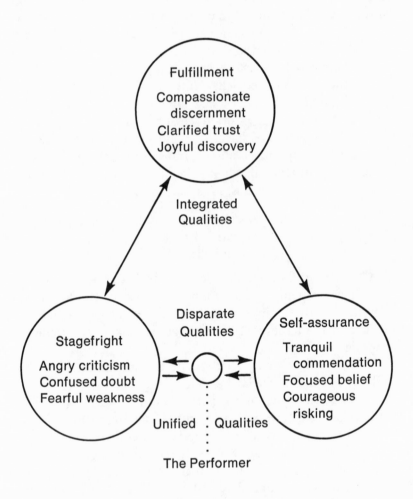

actuality. Together they produce an essence of fulfillment. And finally we come to the major realization—all three of these conceptual levels happen simultaneously. We see three realities taking place at the same time.

Since these three perceptions converge on the focal point of the performer's matrix, the performer, thus centered, receives a new illumination. He or she sees a reality beyond integration—an integral design that not only surpasses the essence of the disparate parts, but also one that preserves the independent integrity of these disparate parts.

Thus, the performer sees stagefright not only as a discrete and viable entity, but also as a higher order of reality—namely, he or she sees it as fulfillment. Fulfillment has stagefright in it; but conversely, fulfillment, being the integrated quality of the collective parts, is likewise at the core of stagefright. That is what is revealed when the performer enters the block of stagefright, embraces it, and passes through to the other side. The two come together into a point beyond integration. With that, the moment is magic.

PART TWO

The Practice

CHAPTER 10

Attuning the Body

Now that we have an idea about the *process* of the stage-fright response, we want to find a workable means to bring what we have discovered to realization. We now turn our attention to practical considerations, describing various procedures we can take to navigate the stagefright block.

Thus far we have talked about the block primarily from the standpoint of thoughts and feelings. We have seen evidence, however, that certain attitudes generate various physical symptoms of stagefright. Indeed, many of the physical symptoms of stagefright originate in the head. But we must say the opposite as well.

The body influences thoughts and feelings. If we furrow our brows into scowls, or clench our fists into tight knots, very soon we will conjure up the rumblings of anger. In contrast, if we skip blithely down the street (how many of us have done *that* lately?), we will be hard-pressed to find fault with anything around us. Consequently, since the physical state of our bodies can be a determining factor in our level of stagefright, we need to consider this point in our discussion, seeing the physical symptoms of stagefright and finding ways to help relieve these effects. Thus in this chapter and the next, we will talk mainly about physical matters. Specifically we first want to learn how to attune our bodies, because a body that is attuned encourages thoughts and feelings that are equally attuned.

This means, however, that we must suspend for the moment our discussion of subpersonalities and emotional energy, and speak instead about kinesthetic sense, or physical sensations in the body. Later (in chapter 12), we can resume our former discussion and, incorporating physical aspects into the total picture, arrive at an integrated approach to stagefright.

Earlier, we likened the stagefright response to the fight-or-flight instinct and brought out the fact that, although this instinct arises in reaction to a threat against life, stagefright arises from a threat to self-concept, not vital existence. Even so, a dramatic shift of body energies takes place to prepare for protective action, thus producing an array of physical symptoms. The muscles throughout the body contract, priming it to spring with a burst of energy (either to flee or fight). In this contraction, the neck muscles pull the head down and the shoulders up, while the back muscles draw the spine into a concave curve. This in turn retracts the pelvis, pulling the genitals up in a vestigial protection reaction. The blood vessels constrict and the blood pressure elevates, heating up the entire mechanism. In an effort to cool the system down, perspiration is released. But since the blood is not flowing freely through the constricted vessels, especially at the extremities, the sweat is cold. Nevertheless, the heart works overtime to get blood to these areas and in so doing causes the face to become flushed. Thus we have cold, clammy hands, yet at the same time feel hot under the collar.

The need for oxygen increases as does our breathing rate, but with the diaphragm muscle shortened, our breaths are shallow and irregular. Eyesight is also distorted. Our pupils dilate to get a broader visual perspective, but this causes vision to be un-focused, a reason we sometimes lose our place when reading. To compound the entire problem, brain-wave frequency increases. The individual feels overwhelmed and confused, as if too many data are coming into the head. Things seem to be happening too fast, and to compensate, the individual tends to speed up—speak too fast, rush tempos, and the like. Increased brain-wave activity changes the entire sense of timing and pacing, so that a variety of miscalculations are likely to surface.

Surveying these various symptoms, we can conclude that one means of handling the block of stagefright is by neutralizing its physical effect. This entails elongating muscles, opening electrical blocks, regulating breathing, reducing brain-wave activity, and, above all, developing a keen kinesthetic awareness so that we know what neutralizing steps can be taken. To this end we have organized the Five-Day Program for performers.

The goal of the Five-Day Program is threefold: first, to give the performer a greater kinesthetic sense of the body; second, to promote advanced relaxation; and third, to show how to build from a state of advanced relaxation into the energy needed for performance. The program is best practiced in at least two cycles, ten days prior to a performance. The time required for practice is about fifteen minutes per day (after the techniques have become familiar). Some may find it helpful to prerecord the directions on tape. In going through the exercises, it will be helpful to keep several points in mind. First, view each session as an awareness experience rather than a group of calisthenic exercises to be performed with gripping determination. Take time to sense how the body feels inside. Never force. Simply feel the movements pleasurably. Second, pay particular attention to the breath so that it flows in a continuous cycle. Last, use the time to explore the body, to gain new knowledge and respect for the way in which it serves performance. The body is our vessel for performance. Let us allow it to aid in that function.

THE FIVE-DAY PROGRAM

The exercises of the first three days are done in a prone position, while those of the last two are done standing. In all descriptions, each set of directions is referred to as an exercise. Since for some the term *exercise* implies repetitive, rote activity, these may be more appropriately perceived of as kinesthetic toning experiences. For the sake of convenient reference, however, the shorter term *exercise* will be used.

Day One

Exercise 1. Preliminary Body Scan.* This exercise provides the basic awareness process which will be cited throughout the program.

Find a quiet place with a soft rug and lie down on your back, with arms parallel to the body, palms down, legs extended, and the feet comfortably apart about six to eight inches. Let the floor support the whole body. Close your eyes and rest a moment. Feel how your head lies on the floor. Is it turned to the left or right a bit? Where is the contact point on the back of the head—in the center or to one side? Make no changes or judgments, simply observe. Notice the space between the neck and the floor. Estimate the size of the space. Move your attention to the shoulders and their contact with the carpet. Is one shoulder higher than the other? Is there pressure at a particular spot, or is the weight evenly distributed? Again, make no changes; just notice. Let your attention travel down your upper arms. Linger a moment at the elbows and feel how they touch the carpet. Proceed down the forearms to the wrists and, as with the neck, sense the space between the wrists and the floor. Observe the palms, then the fingers. Are they warm or cold?

---

*This exercise, and those involving physical motion in the prone position, are derived from techniques developed by Moshe Feldenkrais and described in his book, *Awareness through Movement* (New York: Harper and Row, 1977). Several others have been evolved from various yoga techniques.

Experience the sensations of each finger individually. Is one more curved than another? Do they touch each other?

Now return to the top of the spine, and with the same detailed awareness gradually glide down the spine, noticing how it touches the floor. Get a mental picture of the shape of your spine by the way it feels in relation to the carpet. Give particular attention to the space between the waist and the floor. (If the space here is large enough to produce discomfort in the small of the back and undue pressure on the coccyx, the tail bone at the base of the spine, gently press the coccyx into the rug and release. You can also experiment with bending the knees, placing the soles of the feet on the floor. Later, the tension causing this pressure will gradually be released.)

Move on to the pelvic area. Where is the strongest contact made? Travel slowly down the legs. Feel the thighs, the space behind the knees, the calves, ankles, and feet. Notice if one foot rests at more of an angle than the other. Sense the whole body as an integrated unit and relax.

Exercise 2. Horizontal Neck Rolls. This exercise loosens and elongates neck muscles. Stay on the floor and begin to turn the head slowly from side to side as if you were floating in the ocean. Go as far to each side as is comfortable and "feel" the tension dissolving into the waters. After about fifteen or twenty rolls, experiment with a faster movement and perhaps a wider arc, but without forcing.

Fold the arms across your chest as though hugging yourself. Repeat the head rolls and notice any changes. Does the head turn more easily with arms folded? Swap the arm positions; that is, put the top arm on the bottom and vice versa. Hug yourself in this so-called nonhabitual position. Turn the head again and see if there is a difference. Rest. Return the arms to their original position alongside the body. Sense the neck and observe if the space behind the neck has changed.

Exercise 3. Downward Stretch. Still lying on the carpet, push the palms of the hands along the rug toward the feet and sense a gentle tugging in the shoulders. Release and repeat ten times. Notice the breathing pattern that is created as you do the movement. Alternate the movement, pushing first the left palm toward the feet, then the right. After ten repetitions, incorporate neck rolls. As the left palm pushes toward the feet allow the head to turn to the left; then as the right palm moves down, turn the head to the right. Explore turning the head left as the right palm stretches down and vice versa. Is this movement easier or more difficult than the preceding one? Play around with both. Always be aware of the breathing pattern that grows out of the movements. Relax.

Push the left palm toward the feet and simultaneously stretch the left leg so that it extends several inches longer than the right leg. Repeat the same movement with the right side and alternate the stretches about ten times. Gradually add neck rolls to the movement so that when the left side is stretched, the head turns left, also. Next, counter the stretches by turning the head in the opposite direction from the stretch. After about ten of these movements, rest a moment. Then begin to push the *right* palm toward the feet and extend the *left* leg, and vice versa. After that, incorporate neck rolls. Experiment with various combinations of movements:

- Stretch left arm, left leg; turn head to the left.
- Stretch right arm, right leg; turn head to the right.
- Stretch left arm, left leg; turn head to the right.
- Stretch right arm, right leg; turn head to the left.
- Stretch left arm, right leg; turn head to the right.
- Stretch right arm, left leg; turn head to the left.
- Stretch right arm, left leg; turn head to the right.
- Stretch left arm, right leg; turn head to the left.

Enjoy yourself!

Find the most comfortable movement among those above and repeat with increasing vigor so that the body feels like a snake on its back. Notice particularly the movements of the head, neck, shoulders, and pelvis. Let the carpet massage the entire backside of your body. Rest.

Finish the session by scanning the body as at the beginning. Discover any change in inner sensations? It may feel warmer. Observe if the body lies differently on the floor. Day by day as tension is released, the space between the carpet and the neck, the wrists, the small of the back, and the back of the knees will grow smaller. Even the slightest decrease signals the loosening of tension. Gradually the body will lie flatter, making firmer contact with the floor. When you are ready to get up after the Body Scan, do so slowly to avoid dizziness.

Day Two

Exercise 1. Dead Repose. This exercise induces advanced relaxation by conscious tensing of the muscles and subsequent release.

Lie in the same position as on Day One, except this time turn the palms toward the ceiling. Take a few moments to allow your body to settle into the carpet and your breathing to become calm and regular. With each inhalation, gradually tense the muscle groups listed below. Be sure that all other muscles remain relaxed. With each exhalation gradually release the tension.

- Eyebrows: raise on the inhalation; lower on the exhalation.
- Lips: tighten lips and tongue; release.
- Jaw: tighten jaw; let the lips part a bit on the release.
- Neck: lift head slightly; relax.
- Left arm: tighten first the fingers, then the hand, wrist, forearm, and upper arm; release in reverse order.
- Right arm: same.
- Chest: tighten the muscles under the arms; release.
- Lower abdomen: tighten the muscles without interfering with the breathing process; release.
- Buttocks: tighten the muscles so that the hips are lifted somewhat; release.

- Left leg: begin with the toes and work up through the ankles, calves, knees, and thighs; release in reverse order.
- Right leg: same.
- Entire body: tense and relax.

Lie quietly for a few minutes.

Exercise 2. Horizontal Shoulder Relaxation. This exercise loosens muscles in the neck, shoulders, and upper back. Do each movement about ten times.

Extend hands toward the ceiling. Bend the arms at the elbows and grasp each elbow with the opposite hand. Your arms should form a vertical square to the chest. Move elbows from right to left toward the floor. Keep the movement in the shoulders only. The back stays flat. Stop. Note which forearm is on the bottom. Put it on top, forming the square with the non-habitual grasp, and repeat.

Switch the arms back to the habitual position and continue the movement. Allow the head to move in the same direction as the elbows. Repeat, moving the head in the opposite direction. Which movement is easier? Rest.

Raise the arms toward the ceiling and clasp the hands together with fingers interlocked. Lower the arms to the left, toward the floor. Keep elbows straight, but bend the left wrist to facilitate the movement. Keep the shoulders mainly flat. In the lowered position the only muscles held tense are those in the left arm. All others remain passive, especially those in the right shoulder, which is gently stretched. Check to see if the buttocks are relaxed. Return to starting position and repeat. (See figure 10.1.)

In the same position, lower to the right. Return and repeat several times.

Still in the same position, move alternately from left to right toward the floor. Gradually allow the head to turn with the movement. Next, experiment with holding the head still. Then

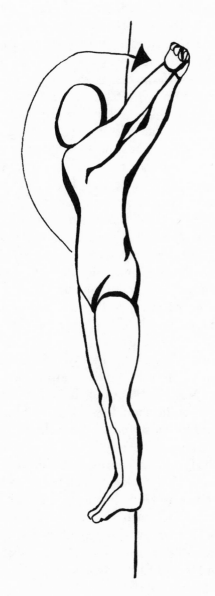

Figure 10.1. The Shoulder Stretch

move the head in the opposite direction. Finish with the easiest head movement. After that, rest.

Repeat the sequence without bending the wrists. Allow the upper body to roll a little more. Rest.

Raise the arms toward the ceiling, with the wrists limp. Lift the shoulders off the floor, stretching the shoulder blade area, then gently rap the shoulders on the floor. Repeat ten times.

In the same position, but with the wrists straight, begin to draw circles with the arms, holding the elbows straight. Make small circles at first and draw them slowly. Reverse the direction. Gradually draw larger circles, moving a bit faster. Explore all kinds of circles: parallel movement, contrary motion, clockwise, counterclockwise, small, large, small ones in one hand, large ones in the other, etc. Let the rest of the body be totally relaxed and sense what is happening to the back of the head, the pelvis, and the legs. Stop and rest. (See figure 10.2.)

Raise the arms toward the ceiling and imagine holding a pencil in the fingers of each hand. Make very fast, small vibration movements with the "pencils." Keep the wrists stiff so that the vibration carries down the arms into the upper torso. Allow the vibrations to grow a bit, and feel that the vibrations originate in the wrists rather than from the finger tips. Sense the difference in the torso. Next, feel that the vibrations emanate from the elbows, then from the shoulders. Different focal points for the vibrations (fingers, wrists, elbows, and shoulders) produce slightly different tingles in the torso.

Still holding the imaginary pencils, turn the vibration movement into small, very fast circles. As before, begin to make all kinds of circles, but here keep the movements small and fast, and the wrists stiff. The rest of the body is totally passive so that the arm motion travels throughout the body from the head, neck shoulders, back, pelvis (notice this especially), and all the way down the legs to the toes. Rest and feel the sensations in your body.

On the vibration movement the body will feel like shaking

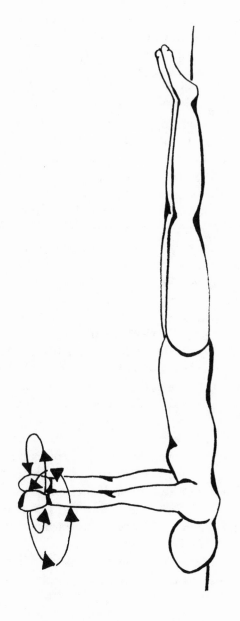

Figure 10.2.   Shoulder Circles

jelly. With the fast circles the body moves in waves, sometimes twisting, other times drifting. Allow all parts to move freely.

Form a vertical square with your arms, as at the beginning of the exercise, and repeat step 1 with light, quick, and nimble movements.

Exercise 3. Hip Relaxation. Still lying on the floor, turn the outside of the right foot toward the floor and return to starting position. Repeat ten times and feel the movement in the hip socket, not the ankle. Then turn the inside of the right foot toward the floor and back straight several times. Next, move the right foot to the left and right.

Bend the right knee toward the ceiling, placing the sole of the foot on the floor. Let the right knee sink to the right as far as it will fall, the foot turning to its side. Return to the upright position. Continue the movement up and down. Exhale as the knee moves to the floor and inhale as it returns to the upright position. As the knee is raised to the starting position, experiment several times with two different senses in making the movements. First, pull the leg up with the muscle that connects the inside of the thigh with the groin (the adductor longus). Next, feel as though the knees were attached to an imaginary string from the ceiling that pulls the leg up, as if the leg floats to the top. Which way is easier? Which uses more muscles in the buttocks?

Begin with both knees bent and follow the same sequence as above, lowering the right knee only. Next, with both knees bent as before, draw the right knee toward the chest, then return to starting position. Repeat several times. If the rest of the body is relaxed, the movement of the knee will be transferred to the chin, head, neck, and shoulders. Notice the breath induced by the movement. (See figure 10.3.)

With knees still bent, begin to make circles with the right knee (lift the right foot off the floor a bit). Reverse the direc-

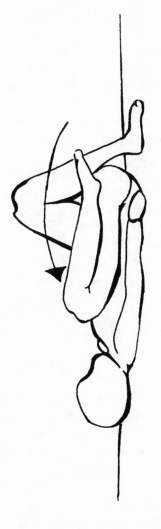

Figure 10.3. Knee to Chest

tion of the circle. Little by little draw larger circles, finally sweeping the knee almost to the floor. Keep the movement located mainly in the hip with the knee joint held stationary at first, and moving only slightly to accommodate the larger circles.

Rest and extend the legs to the original position and compare the left and right sides. Does the right side feel longer than the left? Is it warmer or does it make firmer contact with the floor? Any of these sensations indicates both an elongation of muscles and an opening of channels in the body's electrical system. Slowly get up and walk around to test the difference in the two sides.

You may repeat the entire Hip Relaxation sequence for the left side, or simply leave the two sides unbalanced so that they may be compared. In this way the right side can begin to teach the left by kinesthetic comparison. Or, you may balance the left side by performing the movements only in your imagination; that is, by thinking through the movements slowly, recalling each sensation, but without making the outward gestures. Actually, any of the exercises, once physically experienced, can be done in the imagination. Although it demands acute mental discipline, this procedure produces powerful results, and with fewer repetitions.

Day Three

Begin this session with a Body Scan as in Day One. If you wish, you may move through each area a little more quickly than before. Follow the Body Scan with a few head turns to loosen the neck before beginning the day's session. (Remember, in the Body Scans, turn the palms toward the carpet. This makes it easier to discover the degree of tension present in the wrist. However, the palms face the ceiling in the Dead Repose exercise from Day Two and in another to be detailed for Day Three, the Breathing Body. The object here is to form a straight line from the shoulders to the back of each hand so that the electrical blocks can be opened more easily.)

Exercise 1. Full Horizontal Stretch. Extend the arms over the head with the backs of the hands touching the carpet, or coming as close to it as you comfortably can. Place the left arm so that it continues the same line of the right leg, and align the right arm similarly with the left leg. Begin to stretch the arms alternately, pushing first the left hand along the carpet, then the right. In this position proceed through the same sequence as that of the Downward Stretch exercise outlined in Day One, gradually adding leg stretches and head turns.

Exercise 2. Vertical Arcs. This exercise follows the same intent as that of the Shoulder Relaxation exercise from Day Two.

Start with the arms at the sides, palms down. Raise arms up and over the head, landing with the back of the palms on the carpet. Move easily back and forth through the arc. Then begin faster movements, almost like pitching the arms up and flopping them to the floor. Note what happens to the back, pelvis, legs, and feet. Alternate the arm movements and toy around with different qualities of motion: vigorous, lazy, strong, weak, etc. (See figure 10.4.)

Exercise 3. Elongating Neck and Upper Back. Raise the head enough to reach behind it with both hands and interlace the fingers. Cradle the head in the clasped palms. Relax the elbows, letting them fall toward the carpet. Rest a moment. Then imagine strings from the ceiling attached to the elbows, pulling them up vertically. Allow all twenty pounds of the head to be pulled up slowly as high as the head will easily go. The elbows will almost meet in the raised position. Release slowly and rest. Repeat, interlacing the fingers in the nonhabitual way. Repeat the same movement with the knees bent and the soles of the feet on the floor. Do this sequence slowly and with only one or two repetitions in each position.

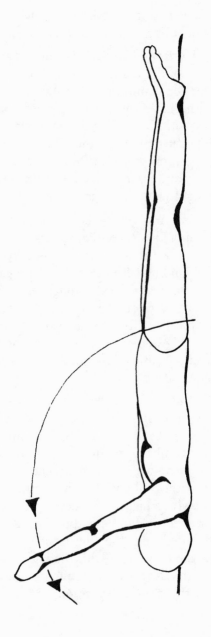

Figure 10.4. Vertical Arcs

Exercise 4. Pelvic Stretch. This exercise loosens and elongates muscles of the lower back. It and the following exercise should be done only after warming up.

Bend the knees as before, with the soles of the feet on the floor; then cross the right leg over the left. Let both knees sink to the right, down as far as is comfortable. Rest there a moment and return. Continue several times; then proceed similarly for the other side, crossing the left leg over the right and sinking to the left. Return to the first position and sink to the right as before. Remain in this position. Interlace the fingers behind the head as in the previous exercise and slowly raise the head with the hands cradled as before. Release and rest. Do the same, allowing the knees to sink to the left side (crossing the left leg over the right).

Exercise 5. Extended Pelvic Stretch. Place the arms outstretched at shoulder level with palms up. Bend the right knee and place the sole of the foot on the floor. Raise the right knee, and, reaching it over the left leg, move it downward toward the floor. Keep the shoulders flat on the floor so that the lower torso twists. Do not force. Go as far as you comfortably can and stop. Relax the shoulders, back, and pelvis; then return to starting position. Repeat once or twice. In time, as you progress and are able to make knee contact with the floor, move the contact point to the level of the thighs and hips, and even higher if possible. In the higher positions the shoulders may raise a bit off the floor. To add greater stretch to the twist, turn the head to the right. Proceed similarly with the other side. (See figure 10.5.)

Exercise 6. The Breathing Body. This exercise reduces tension in the diaphragm and facilitates your ability to sense the body's electrical energy system.

Lie on your back as before with palms turned up. Take a few moments to observe your body, then turn your attention to your breathing. Sense how the air feels in your nostrils as you

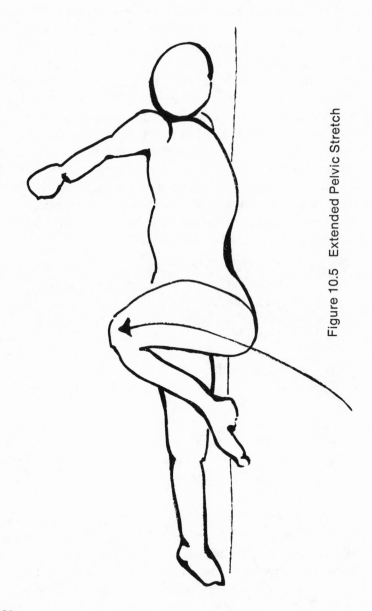

Figure 10.5 Extended Pelvic Stretch

breathe in and out. Are they cool on the inhalation and warm on the exhalation? Place your left hand on the abdomen, just below the navel and begin to lengthen the breaths. As you inhale, count silently and slowly to four. Each count represents a little less than a second. Exhale at the same pace and establish this pattern: inhale—two—three—four; exhale—two—three—four. Think of your breath as circular in direction so that the gap between breaths is closed as much as possible and the breath flows continuously. As you inhale, feel the left hand on the abdomen being buoyed up, and as you exhale feel it floating down. Take the time that you need to establish a natural rhythm, then return the left hand to the side, palm up.

Now imagine that you breathe in, between the eyebrows and out the nostrils. Feel the cooling sensation of the breath as it enters between the eyebrows and the warming feeling as it leaves the nostrils. After you gain this perception, keep breathing in between the eyebrows, and in a step-by-step progression, imagine that you are in turn breathing out the areas listed below. Linger at each area for at least three complete breaths. Be aware of any changes in sensations that take place as the breath enters between the eyebrows, moves down the body and out of the spot designated below:

1. Mouth
2. Neck
3. Down the shoulders, arms, and out the fingers
4. Heart
5. Navel
6. Genitals
7. Anus
8. Down the entire body and out the feet

To heighten the feeling of breath flowing through the body, you may want to "see" vapor coming out the exhaling parts. Next, imagine that your entire body is a huge sponge, every pore breathing in and out. Pause.

After several moments, imagine that you can *see* yourself performing. Take time to get a clear picture and when you have it, assert to yourself three times, in a strong, deliberate, silent voice, "I see myself to be calm and alert." Then fancy that you actually are performing. In your imagination stand before the audience and assert three times, "I *feel* calm and alert." Lie there a moment and discover how it feels to be calm and alert. This entire sequence combines a breathing exercise, a quasi-meditative state, and an autogenetic suggestion. The three elements may be used separately or in combination.

The Breathing Body exercise, with or without the autogenetic suggestion, will prove to be one of the most valuable tools for the performer. Practice of this exercise can neutralize a myriad of stagefright symptoms. Most notably it reduces brain wave activity, thus bringing the diffused mind into clearer focus. In addition, it allows muscles to "let go," whereby energy channels are opened. Even on first experience the performer will feel deeply relaxed and may notice tiny shifts of energy in the areas where the breath is "exhaled." (A personal note: I have done this exercise when "hooked up" to a bio-feedback machine; although I have no great skills at performing so-called mind control feats, I have been able, through this exercise, to increase the temperature in my fingers by ten degrees. I also credit practice of this exercise as being a major factor in allowing me years ago to stop taking drugs for high blood pressure.)

Day Four

Exercise 1. Upright Body Scan. This exercise uses the same procedure as that in the Preliminary Body Scan, except here the emphasis is placed on finding a natural standing posture.

In a standing position, proceed through the detailed Body Scan as described in Day One. Start with the head and move through every area of the body down to the toes. This time make any posture adjustments that add to a comfortable stance. Experiment with standing a little pigeon-toed (toes pointed inward) and see if this opens the muscles in the buttocks and around the anus. Subsequently, point the toes straight and find an easy position, with the feet comfortably apart and the weight of the body evenly distributed over the entire bottom surface of the feet.

Some individuals equate standing straight with an exaggerated military stance in which the shoulders are plunged back, the chest is thrust up and out, and the chin clamped down on the chest. From earlier observations about the influence of stagefright on posture, we can see that this stance, with its acute muscle contractions, in effect abets stagefright symptoms. All the muscles of the back and neck are shortened and the spine is compressed into an "S" shape. The shoulders and upper back are thrust back of center and receive no support from below. In fact, the entire support structure lists out of kilter so that none of the body's components stack up on top of each other. Since natural support is lacking, the upper torso is held up by straining back muscles which eventually give out, leaving one with a "bad" back (figure 10.6).

Rather than freezing into this ungainly hero's stance, imagine that the back elongates into a subtle convex curve that begins at the nape of the neck and ends at the back of the knees, which are bent slightly. In this position the shoulders hang naturally, the chest expands freely, and the pelvis tilts a bit forward, cradling the organs it holds. A good foundation supports the head, which floats easily in a balanced position, neither tilted down, up, nor to the side. The overall inward feeling is one of resting down into the floor and floating up at the same time. Countering the influence of stagefright, this natural stance allows muscles to expand easily, affording a fluid accessibility in which movements can be executed swiftly and with economy. The body stands willingly poised for any kind of action (figure 10.7).

Exercise 2. Flutter Breathing. In the same comfortable standing position, take very shallow breaths through the nose, as fast as you can flutter in and out, like panting. Do this for about six

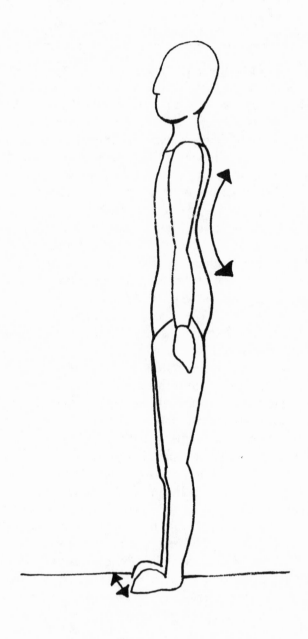

Figure 10.6. Hero's Posture

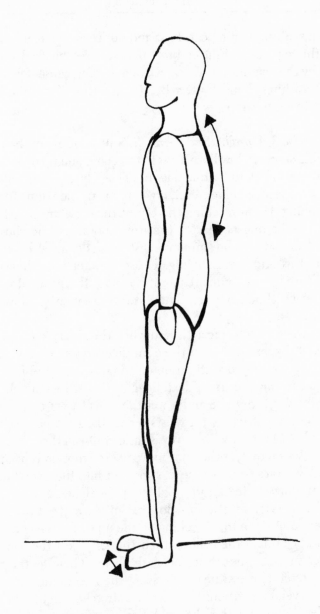

Figure 10.7.   Natural Stance

seconds. Stop, then repeat. Rest and notice any changes in the breathing process. Flutter breathing releases blocked energy held by the diaphragm, which, when held taut, causes fast, shallow breathing. Thus, Flutter Breathing restores longer, deeper cycles to the breath.

Exercise 3. Upright Body Stretch. Still standing in the comfortable stance, allow both arms to travel out and up toward the ceiling, tracing a full semicircle. Inhale as the arms rise, and as they approach shoulder level, gradually turn the palms toward the ceiling. Upon reaching the top of the arc above the head, interlace the fingers. Stretch the arms, shoulders, and chest up as high as you can and simultaneously push downward with the pelvis, legs, and feet. Exhaling, release the stretch and lower the arms through the semicircular arc. Rotate the palms down as they reach shoulder level. The entire movement is slow and smooth.

See what muscles are activated when the arms are raised and lowered. Experiment with three subtle changes in muscle activation. First, put your attention on the shoulders and feel that they are raising the arms. Next, imagine that strings attached to the elbows gently raise and lower the arms. After that, attach the imaginary strings to the wrists and let the arms leisurely float up and coast down. Which way is easiest? On all the raises have the sensation that, as the arms move up, the motion is balanced by a downward thrust of the legs and feet into the floor. On the return, allow the feet to grow lighter on the floor.

After several repetitions, do not interlace the fingers but rather point them to the ceiling on the upward stretch. Stretch the right arm to the ceiling, then the left. Feel the shoulder blades massage the tissues beneath them. Then, as the right arm stretches, press the right leg on the floor, and vice versa. After several repetitions, do alternate stretches: right arm with left leg, left arm with right leg. Relax and observe if the shoulders are lower and the neck feels longer.

Exercise 4. Shoulder Raises and Circles. Still standing, raise the shoulders slowly. Inhaling, try to touch them to the ears. Hold for a moment; then, exhaling, let the hands become weights which slowly and gently pull the shoulders down as far as they will comfortably go. Repeat eight to ten times. Begin to move the shoulders in a circular motion. Start small and gradually expand the circumference of the circles. Reverse the direction. Any jerkiness that interrupts a smooth flow indicates tension. Give emphasis to these sensitive spots, working gently back and forth through them. Now follow the same procedure moving only one shoulder while the other remains totally relaxed.

Exercise 5. The Windmill. Find plenty of room so that you can swing your arms in full circles like a windmill. Begin with your arms at your sides. Sling the arms up and out in front, over the head, back, and down full circle. Start gently. As you grow more limber (this may take several sessions) increase the speed and force of the circles, up to about eighty per minute, so that when the arms whiz down behind, the heels will be lifted slightly off the floor (figure 10.8).

Now reverse the direction of the circle. Later, experiment with various kinds of circular motion: parallel, contrary, clockwise, counterclockwise. Try starting with one hand at the top, the other by the side. Relax. (Note: if you have bursitis or arthritis in the shoulder, the Windmill can be particularly useful in loosening tendons and joints. But *never overexert!* You may break a bone or dislocate your shoulder. Begin with half-windmills, swinging only through the bottom half of the circle. And use caution and common sense.)

Exercise 6. The Corkscrew. The source of movement for this exercise initiates in the legs and pelvis, and spirals into the shoulders and arms like a corkscrew. The entire upper torso remains passive, allowing the energy from below to swing it freely.

Begin with the feet 14 to 18 inches apart and pointed straight

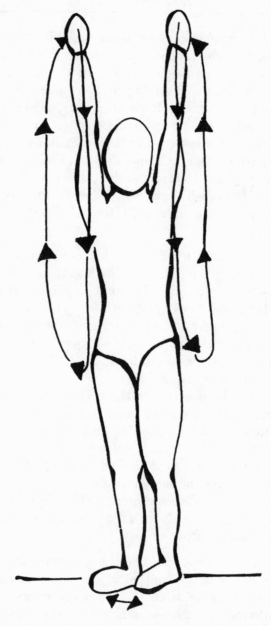

Figure 10.8. The Windmill

out. Quickly thrust the pelvis counterclockwise to the right, pressing the right leg back and the left leg forward, but without actually moving the feet off the floor. Allow the upper torso to remain completely passive. The lower thrust carries the upper torso with it and the arms swing in consequence. Reverse the motion, thrusting clockwise to the left. When you get the idea, thrust right and left, gradually increasing the force. Pause long enough between thrusts for the upper body to catch up. Eventually, the arms should swing so freely that at the pause they slap the body on the point of contact. Rest and sense the inner activity (figure 10.9).

Exercise 7. The Body Shake. Pretend that you have a sticky substance on the ends of your fingers and that you are determined to get it off. To do so, begin to flick the wrists vigorously, leaving the fingers totally passive. Get faster and faster, turning the flicks into gyrations so rapid that the fingers blur and feel as though they might be flung from the hand. Bring the elbows into action and begin flapping them like an excited bird. Move on to the shoulders so that they and the entire arm shake excitedly. Begin to shake the head in every direction. Let the tongue hang out. Step by step carry the excitement down the body—into the chest, abdomen, pelvis (giving special attention here), thighs, and knees. Last, stamp the feet on the floor. Now the whole body is in wild abandon. A sound may want to come out—an Ohhh, an Ahh, perhaps a scream. Allow that to happen.

By degrees let the body begin to calm down. Take enough time so that the body directs you in the slowing down process. When it has finished all the shaking, close the eyes and take inventory of the entire body. You will feel tingly and relaxed at the same time. Enjoy this for a few moments. Then, still with the eyes closed, imagine that you can see yourself in a performance situation as you did yesterday. With an inward voice of quiet assurance, assert to yourself three times, "I see myself to be calm and vibrant." Then, without physically moving, feel as

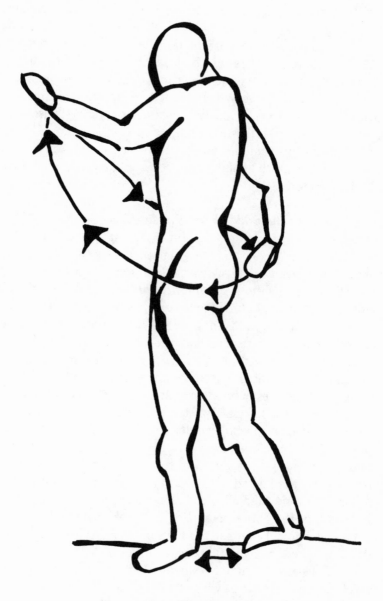

Figure 10.9.   The Corkscrew

though you are actually performing and affirm three times, "I feel myself to be calm and vibrant." Take some time for this process, then slowly open your eyes.

Exercise 8. Walking Body Scan. Without interruption, begin walking around the room to see how you move when you feel calm and vibrant. Do a complete body inventory from head to toe as you walk. Notice particularly how the various parts of the body move, especially the shoulders and pelvis. See how your feet make contact with the floor. Do they inscribe with each step a circular motion, a back-and-forth motion, or an up-and-down motion? Is there anything about your walking at present that needs changing in order to suggest calm vibrancy more clearly?

Ultimately, the walking posture that will evolve is one in which the lower half of the body settles calmly downward, feeling grounded in the earth. The chest and head, resting on this foundation, seem to float upward so that the upper torso feels vibrantly expanded. The shoulders, however, do not rise, but rest easily on the expanded rib cage; and the spine suggests a gentle, convex curve as mentioned previously. In walking, the ankles will be limber and the feet will contact the floor heel first, then roll to the toe, but this contact is almost simultaneous. Your steps, rather than clumping up and down, will inscribe an ever-so-slight circular motion. As you walk, you may picture pedaling a bicycle, but the circular movement is much more subtle than this. Adding to the gait, the hands will swing freely, countering the motion of the steps; that is, as the left foot steps forward, the right hand will swing to the front, and vice versa. Take pleasure in the way you walk and discover how the feeling of calm vibrancy is disclosed in your stride.

Day Five

Choose one of the previous body inventory examples—the prone or upright Body Scan, the Dead Repose sequence, or the

Breathing Body exercise—and proceed through the complete sequence.

Exercise 1. Neck Rolls. Standing in the posture described in Day Four, imagine that the head floats like a ball bearing on the shoulders and begin to roll it slowly in a clockwise direction. Start with the head tilted forward and exhale. As you begin the circle, inhale. At the point where the head is tilted back, begin to exhale. After several times, reverse the direction. Keep the circle's circumference small at first so that the movement is easy and smooth. Gradually let the circumference grow without force. If there is jerkiness in the movement, return to the center and sink into the affected spot easily. Then with little effort move back and forth through the sensitive area.

Exercise 2. Dangling Head Turns. Bend forward and place the hands on the knees, which are slightly bent. Let all twenty pounds of the head dangle and begin to turn from left to right as if gesticulating "no." Try different speeds in turning and find one that feels right. Keep the breath flowing and relax into the bend. Slowly begin to unbend, but allow the head still to dangle, saying "no" as the spine straightens. Bring the head to the upright position last. Stop the turning and relax. Repeat three or four times, sometimes letting the hands dangle rather than resting them on the knees. (See figure 10.10.)

Exercise 3. Bouncing Bend. Bend over as before and allow both the head and the hands to dangle freely like dead weights. Here, let the head, shoulders, and arms feel heavier than in the Dangling Head Turns. Bend the knees, then straighten them in an easy, bouncing fashion. Do nothing with the upper torso; permit the activity of the knees to travel through the pelvis and be transferred by chain reaction to the upper torso, which remains completely passive. Experiment both with the speed of

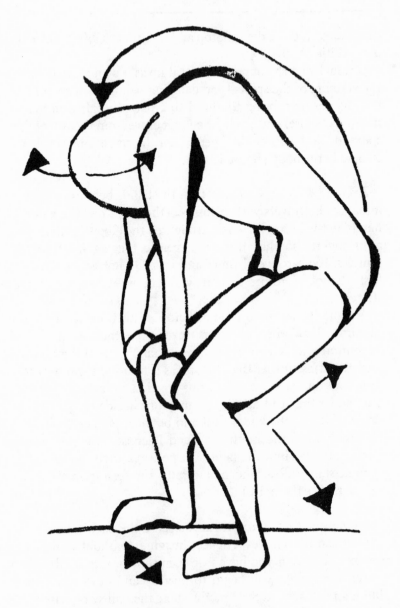

Figure 10.10.   Dangling Head Turns

the bounce and the depth. Stop and rest, maintaining the bent-over position.

Gradually let the upper torso float up as if being lifted by the top vertebra of the spine, head dangling behind. Finally, in the upright position, bring the head to a natural, balanced placement. As before, sense a slight convex curve from the top of the spine to the backs of the knees. Feel the sensations you have created in the body (figure 10.11).

Exercise 4. Back Stretch. Reach the hands behind the back, interlace the fingers with palms together, and rest the clasped hands on the buttocks. Then, straighten the elbows and lift the arms slightly so that there is a gentle tugging in the back muscles. Repeat several times and rest. Do not go too high at first, though in future sessions you may want to increase the stretch.

Assume the same position as before. This time, as you raise the arms, bend the upper torso over from the hips as far as is comfortable, keeping the knees straight. In this position, raise the arms further than before, as if to bring them over the head, but do not strain. Hold this position a moment. Breathe out and let the head dangle, turning it from side to side as if to say "no." Bend the knees a bit and bounce very gently (not as vigorously as in the Bouncing Bend Exercise). Straighten the knees and relax into the bent-over position, then return to the upright stance. Rest and be aware of the feeling in the back muscles. (See figure 10.12.)

Exercise 5. Body Quiver. As you sense the back muscles following the previous experience, imagine (without tightening any muscles) that you have just been thrown into a tub of icy water. Cold chills will begin to play up and down the spine, but maintain repose. See exactly where the chills originate; and intensify the feeling, turning the chills into physical vibrations. Send these vibrations in turn throughout the body, shooting

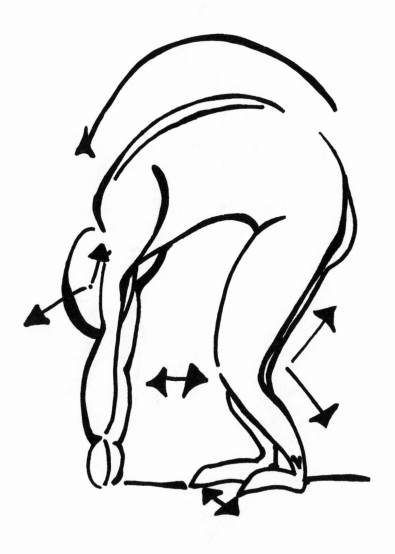

Figure 10.11.   Bouncing Bend

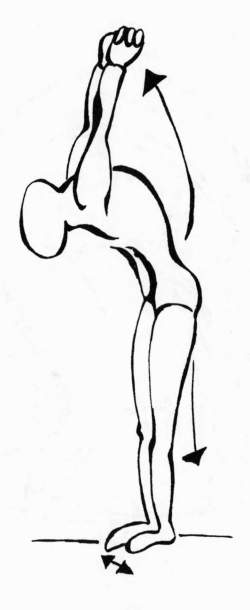

Figure 10.12.   Back Stretch

quivers into the neck, head, shoulders, arms and hands, pelvis, and legs and feet. Allow the body to quiver all over until the energy plays itself out. Rest and see what you feel.

If the vibrating motions have been fairly intense and allowed to subside naturally, you will notice a feeling of composure overlaid with an element of clarity in which the inside of the head feels alive. This mixture of feelings is a kind of quiet brilliance, differing ever so slightly from the calm vibrance after the Body Shake.

Sustain without interruption the inner sensation of quiet brilliance created by the Body Quiver. Now imagine a specific performing situation and this time actually pantomime postures and gestures that convey quiet brilliance. For example, if you are a speaker, pantomime conveying this quality as you are making a speech. How do you stand? What do your hands do as you speak? What supports the weight of the body? Do you weigh more, or less, than usual? Do you stand behind a podium, or not? As a swimmer, how does the water feel on your body when the body is quietly brilliant? How does your body move in the water? Are the strokes longer and slower than usual, faster and shorter, longer and faster, or slower and shorter? What area of the body do the strokes emanate from—shoulders, chest, navel, genitals? In other words, whatever your profession, mime the movements. See how the body feels specifically, and how it moves as it transmits quiet brilliance. During the pantomime, make a detailed body inventory.

The Body Quiver is similar to the Body Shake in that the whole body is brought into intense activity. But while the outward motion of the Quiver is less visible, the inward feeling is more concentrated than in the Shake. Another distinction, the kinesthetic sense created by the Shake grew from a physical action, according to the directions given here. With the Quiver a mental suggestion—icy water—initiated the sensation. Both approaches are useful, making physical movements or giving mental suggestions, since as we know, physical actions stimulate thought patterns and, likewise, mental suggestions influence physical movements.

There is an emotional connection we can make as well. The quiet brilliance produced by the Quiver and the calm vibrance induced by the Shake are qualities quite similar to emotional states we have previously discussed—clarity and tranquility, respectively. Since clarity represents the transformed state of confusion and tranquility denotes the transformed feelings of anger, we can see another practical application of these two exercises. Namely, the Quiver can be used to dissipate confusion, changing its energy to clarity, and the Shake can be called upon to redirect anger into a feeling of (active) tranquility.

Exercise 6. Creating New Sensations. In future sessions, you may want to experiment with other feelings to lay over the fundamental one of repose. For example, brilliance may be inappropriate for the musician playing Chopin's "Funeral March" or the linebacker who wants to bust through a human wall. Perhaps the dancer wants elegance; the musician, compassion; the linebacker, power; the club speaker, joviality. Suffice it to say that energies manifest themselves as body sensations and they are available in an infinite variety of one's choosing. Precisely where energies originate in the body or exactly what a given sensation feels like cannot be described exactly. Perhaps a feeling of playfulness emerges from a dancing tingle behind the eyes; a glow of compassion might radiate from warmth in the breast. Power may find its first rumble with the most subtle impulses in the recesses of the abdomen. The idea is to discover the quality and source of the feeling, then let it spread throughout the body.

Creating a feeling to suit individual needs in performance begins with removing needless tension and replacing it with quiet, relaxed vitality. This is best accomplished after the Body Shake or Body Quiver exercise, since either of these dissipates tension and invigorates the body. As one acquires experience, simply remembering the feeling of shaking or quivering without making the outward gestures will produce the same end. To create new sensations in the beginning, however, go through either the Shake or the Quiver, then follow this plan.

Let the body wind down afterwards and feel the quiet awareness you have generated. Then call to mind a feeling to integrate with this awareness—one valuable to your performance circumstances: joy, humor, daring, power, clarity, vibrance, focus, vitality, compassion, wonder, grandeur, nimbleness, playfulness. Make up your own words. In the relaxed state, see what area of the body begins to stir when the added feeling is evoked. Be still and allow the qualifying sensation to spread through the body, growing and becoming integrated with the state of calmness. Then, pantomime movements of your performance as just explained. Play around with this process and have fun with it.

Having fun, of course, is one of the pleasant features of the entire Five-Day Program. In attuning the body, we discover its innate resources, and this brings a feeling of enthusiasm. More important, it reveals a sense of autonomy. Every experience that increases our body awareness moves us a step closer to our inner power. Learning how to use this power, how to create the specific energy we require, remains an individual process, however; one we discover in our own particular way. Therefore, it is helpful to develop a personal program, to find a plan that works best for us. With that we gain the ability to actualize the power we possess and create the specific energy we need for performance.

CHAPTER 11

Building
a Personal Program

IN GOING THROUGH THE EARLIER exercises, you probably found that the physical symptoms of stagefright can be approached in two contrasting designs: one to neutralize the symptoms, the other to intensify them (for example, the Body Scan as opposed to the Body Shake). In selecting exercises for a personal program, keep both approaches in mind as a means to navigate the block.

A second point in developing a personal program concerns the issue of breathing. No matter which exercises are chosen, be aware that the breathing cycle is an integral part of the process. Breathing is a bridge between the mind, the emotions, and the body, and regulating the breath cycle is the most accessible means of changing kinesthetic states. A scattered mind produces a restless body, and, proportionally, an agitated body provokes a racing mind. In this state, breathing is fast, shallow, and irregular. Consciously calming the breath into long, regular cycles, however, soothes both a restless body and an emotionally charged mind.

153

Kinesthetic sensations undoubtedly constitute the most important factor in establishing a specific plan. Each exercise in the Five-Day Program stimulates different, though subtle indeed, sensations in the body. In developing a plan, above all feel as precisely as possible how each exercise affects the body so that in time you can perceive the slightest nuance in kinesthetic changes. Then you will be able to choose the exercise that gives the exact energy you need. Ultimately, any energy you can create by going through an exercise will be available in performance. That, of course, is the goal of a personal program—to create the specific energy required in performance. It is accomplished by transferring the sensations of the exercises into the performing experience.

The Kinesthetic Transfer

The first step in transferring sensations was given when we suggested pantomiming performance gestures after the Body Quiver. Here are other steps in the kinesthetic transfer.

1. During a rehearsal or training session, stop the action in midstream. For example, speakers, interrupt a sentence; musicians, suspend in midair a musical phrase; athletes and dancers, take a momentary time-out from whatever motions you are executing. Then go through a quick Body Scan, only seconds long. Make any necessary changes, and resume action.

2. Later, progress to a Performing Body Scan. This means taking a body inventory without stopping the rehearsal. Gear your observations to your specific performing function. For instance, notice the shoulders as you carry the ball, sense the buttocks as you sit on the piano bench, feel the breath travel through your vocal chords as you sing or speak. See what is happening in your feet. Are tensions in the neck, shoulders, elbows, or wrists causing cold hands (or feet)? These are suggested observations only. Formulate others

that seem appropriate and follow through with any needed adjustments.

3. The final transfer comes when we approach the kinesthetic transfer from a totally mental orientation, where, by mental recall, one can "flip back" into an attitude originally created during the exercises. Making no physical gestures, an individual simply remembers the feelings created by the gestures. A pianist may want to recall the sensation of breathing out the hands. A dancer might wish to re-create the feeling of calm brilliance experienced after the Body Quiver. Some might choose to "live" in their shoulders a moment and remember how they felt after the Windmill. Although the ability to flip back takes practice, a rich variety of mental recalls await discovery.

Mental recalls, along with the Body Scan and breath regulation, provide the most valuable tools in handling stagefright when the performer is actually before the audience, since he cannot very well interrupt the proceedings to make physical gestures. In addition to these, and equally important to performance, is the climate that one establishes in the thirty minutes or so before an event. Whatever attitude is attained here will be shown in the performance itself. The countdown beforehand is a delicate time, indeed, one requiring judicious attention and preparation.

In the Greenroom

Some performers jokingly refer to the greenroom (the lounge in a theater where performers wait) as the place where many performers "turn green" and more than a few throw up while waiting to go on.* Whether a person waits in the greenroom,

---

*Actually the greenroom got its name from the fact that "at one time the walls were coloured green to relieve the eyes affected by the glare of the stage lights." E. Cobham Brewer, *Dictionary of Phrase and Fable* (New York: Avenal Books, 1870), p. 551.

the locker room, or behind the bandstand, the situation is the same. That half hour is filled with lonely moments. Anticipation charges the air and stagefright reaches a precipitous peak. Some, hopelessly wishing to dispel the clutches of a churning stomach, sit in stony silence. Others fluster through last minute warm-ups in a way that disperses attention. Still others, afraid of losing concentration, stuff themselves with final instructions: "Watch out for those backhands." "Don't push too soon." "Keep the throat open for that high B-flat." We know where these reminders come from!

We know also that none of these approaches will likely prove helpful. What the performer needs is poised energy—eagerness without frenzy, focus without force—not jack-in-the-box suspense, coiled and ready to pop out on cue. He or she needs to reduce brain wave activity, and to unclog the body's electrical system in order to gain focused attention. Lastly, the performer needs to take care of, or at least modify, specific symptoms that may have broken out in the moments of waiting.

To meet these needs, some portion of the Five-Day Program can be called into service, although some modifications may be appropriate. Techniques like the Body Scan, which originally called for lying on the floor, can of course be performed while sitting or standing. Also, any of the exercises can be done with very small, practically invisible movements, if anyone is reluctant to perform the exercises while others are watching. Others watching, however, should present no problem with reference to Breath Regulation and the Body Scan. Both can be done even while talking to others and no one will be the wiser.

With these introductory comments in mind, let us turn to specific techniques that can be used in the greenroom. Most are drawn from the Five-Day Program and are here grouped as aids for particular symptoms. Each group includes neutralizing techniques as well as others that intensify the symptoms. Experiment and see which approach works best, but, in general, conclude with a neutralizing exercise to "tone down" the body. Since most of the techniques have been described earlier, they are given here in checklist form.

SYMPTOMS: Cold hands, cold feet, or leg cramps.
1. Body Shake (localized to the affected limbs, not applied to the whole body).
2. Windmill (for hands).
3. Corkscrew.
4. Breathing Body.
Imagine that you breathe in slowly between the eyebrows and out the hands or feet.

Tension-relaxing exercise (described in the Dead Repose exercise). Clench hands (or feet) as tightly as possible; inhale and try to make the hands get colder. Release; exhale and allow the hands to get warmer.

SYMPTOMS: Body tremors, shaking hands, stomach butterflies.
1. Deep Breathing.
2. Body Shake or Body Quiver (either localized to the affected area or allowed to spread through the body).
3. Mental Recall. Remember a former evoked feeling such as calm vibrance. Let the feeling emanate from the pit of the stomach and spread throughout the entire body.

SYMPTOM: Dry mouth.
1. Make the tongue flabby and wide enough to cover all the bottom teeth. Glide the tongue back and forth over the top of the bottom teeth. Then swirl the tongue quickly around the bottom of the mouth with a darting motion.
2. Inhale and push the tongue against the roof of the mouth. Holding the breath, increase the pressure until the Adam's apple feels as though it will be pulled from its socket. Release, sigh, then swallow.

SYMPTOMS: Diffused thoughts, lack of concentration, pounding heart.
1. Body Scan.
2. Deep Breathing (for about five minutes, counting slowly to four with each inhalation and the same with each exhalation).
3. Flutter Breathing.
4. Breathing Body.

One final comment: Almost any effect of stagefright can be changed by first exaggerating the symptom, whatever it may be, then moving to the exact opposite stance, and finally going back and forth between the opposite states until they either begin to fuse, or the desired quality emerges. For example, if tension crops up in the shoulders, increase the tension gradually and breathe in slowly. Then, gradually release the tension and breathe a slow sigh of relief. Repeat several times.

Kinesthetic knowledge is the fundamental answer in resolving the physical symptoms of stagefright. Such knowledge is gained simply by our observing the body, meaning that we move our awareness to its various parts, perceiving the sensations that exist. Whatever contributes to our observing faculties is a determining factor in developing an individual plan to meet the problems of stagefright.

Thus, we have a number of things to remember in finding a personal program, but they all encourage experiment, so that we find the individual approach that suits our purpose best. And the one that suits us best is the one that enables us not only to alleviate the symptoms of stagefright, but to use and direct stagefright's energy for our benefit.

In these last two chapters we have approached the problem of stagefright in terms of physical symptoms. One symptom that forms an underlying thread to our discussion is that of increased brain-wave activity. All the techniques and suggestions we discussed serve to quiet a diffused mind. Although diffusion occurs because of physiological effects, it crops up also because of psychological concerns. The content of our thoughts determines the mind's state of diffusion or focus as much as does the physical activity of brain waves. So now we can look at the issue from the other viewpoint, from the subjective side of our nature. Not only do we want to consider the content of our thoughts, we want also to carry our program one step further—to find a way in which we can integrate the body with our thoughts and feelings.

CHAPTER 12

Gearing
for Integration

MANY TIMES I HAVE REFERRED to the interdependence of the body, mind, and emotions. They are three separate but intimately related systems that mutually influence each other. Whatever takes place in one is distributed to the other two. This is not to say, however, that the three systems are always totally synchronized. One may be consciously at odds with another. My body may be exhausted, yet my mind filled with restless energy. I may feel one way and think another. And if not at odds consciously, the systems may be in unconscious disagreement, due to a lack of awareness. I may not know the feelings I hold, even though my body sensations describe the state; I may not know what thoughts race through my head, even though my mood could give me a clue. Disagreement among the three systems is characteristic of stagefright. They are so out of synchrony they begin to fight each other for control.

Thus we come to the cumulative point toward which all our discussions have been directed: to find a means by which we can bring all our faculties together into a fusion of forces, and by this pass through the block of stagefright.

To describe this fusion of forces, I have spoken in terms of an "integration" that occurs on several fronts simultaneously: dual opposites; the body, mind, and emotions; the elements in the performer's matrix; and even the performer and his or her performance. Let us remember, however, that integration, in the way I have used the term, means more than a fusion of forces. I described earlier an integral design that comes into being when the performer passes through stagefright and finds himself or herself at the focal point of the performer's matrix —a focal point from which three conceptual modalities are perceived: unity, diversity, and a higher integration of elements.

So to us, integration has special meaning. It denotes a higher level of understanding that evolves from several contexts of reference (in our terminology, from the concurrent reference point of the subpersonalities, the Observing "I," and the Higher Self). Earlier I described this higher level of understanding as "the step beyond." Thus the title of this chapter, "Gearing for Integration," indicates something particular—it means preparing to take this "step beyond."

The chapter contains three major sections. The first offers three exercises using the principles of guided imagery. By experimenting with these, each performer can discover, first, the dynamics of stagefright as they operate uniquely in him or her; second, the dynamics between polar opposites; and third, the dynamics of evoking the High Self. The second and third parts pertain to more specific issues: one being the matter of choice, showing how to strengthen volition; the other being the matter of disturbing thoughts, showing how to respond effectively to conflicting inner voices.

Since all three parts of the chapter are intended to help the performer see how stagefright fits into the larger integral design (see figure 9.1), it is a good idea to keep this design in mind as you read this chapter. That will clarify many points along the way.

GUIDED IMAGERY

Visualizing mental images is one way to bring into conscious awareness certain concepts or attitudes we hold pertaining to performance. Images are a reflection of our attitudes, and these are bound together in various psychological configurations we have labeled subpersonalities. Becoming aware of these subpersonalities puts us in a better position to use their energy at will and to bring into accord those subpersonalities that contradict our purpose.

Each of the following exercises takes roughly twenty minutes. You may wish to read the directions from the book, memorize the outline, or have a friend read the directions to you. Better yet, if possible pre-record the directions, leaving pauses sufficient for you to complete the steps. It is better to repeat each exercise at least once over a period of several days before proceeding to the next. After each session, write down your reactions. Later, as you rehearse, think about the experience and its meaning for your performance.

Another point, since the exercises may involve a new experience, is that you might have fun keeping tabs on any subpersonalities that might be aroused as you read through the directions. The Critic (naturally!) may find them silly, the Doubter might doubt that they could work, and the Weakling may be embarrassed to give them a try. To gain the greatest benefit, keep an attitude of experimentation. Toy with ideas and, above all, enjoy yourself.

Exercise 1. The Performance*

Find a quiet place and either lie on the carpet or sit in a comfortable chair. Close your eyes and take a few moments to listen

---

*These exercises are adapted from various ones administered at the Psychosynthesis Institute in San Francisco and have been modified here to suit the needs specifically of performers. Similar, and more extensive examples can be found in the periodical *Synthesis*, vols. 1, 2, 3, and 4 (830 Woodside Rd., Redwood City, CA 94061).

to your breathing. You may want to go through a quick Body Scan. Let your body relax, and empty your head of disturbing thoughts.

Allow an image of a meadow to emerge; it may be one you know or some other one you have never seen. In either case, the meadow is a peaceful spot, the sun is shining, and the sky is clear. Look around the meadow and see its sights. See the color of the grass. There may be some trees. Listen to the sounds. Maybe some birds are singing. Smell the smells of the meadow. In your mind's eye, walk around and explore the meadow at leisure.

As you walk around, find a path that leads out of the meadow. Begin to meander down this path, taking in the sights. As you proceed down the path, let the thought dawn on you that you are walking to a performance that you are just about to give (whatever "performance" means to you: a lecture, concert, play, game, or something else relevant). Going further down the path, come to a small knoll. On the other side of this knoll and out of·sight is the place where you will perform. As you climb the little knoll, the performance place comes into view; it may be a building or an outdoor arena. Approach slowly and find your way to an entrance, perhaps the front door or front gate, which at the moment is closed. Observe the closed entrance. Although you cannot see behind the entrance, you can hear voices; the audience is already assembled, waiting for you to perform.

Walk up closer to the entrance and stand before it. When you are squarely in front of the entrance, allow it to open so that you can see the people behind it. Watch these people; let them come out and stream by you. Make no judgments; simply observe them as they pass by. Pick out two persons who seem central to the action, who in some way catch your interest. Go up to these two. You may have a question for them; if so, ask it and allow them to answer. Look at their distinguishing features —the way they hold their bodies, the clothes they wear, the sound of their voices. Ask them what they want from you—and why. Next, ask them what they need from you—and why. Notice the difference between their wants and needs.

Choose one of the persons and place him or her directly in front of you. Study the person for a bit, then imagine that you can change places with him or her for a few moments. Actually become this person and look back, as this person, at yourself. Begin to make physical gestures that represent this person's character. How does that individual carry his or her body? What sounds does this person make? As this person, how does the world look to you? What feelings do you feel? Then become yourself and see if the other person has changed in any way. See if anything else needs to be said at this time between the two of you. When your conversation seems complete, bring your awareness back to your surroundings in the room, and in your own time open your eyes.

After you open your eyes, imagine a performance situation. If you can, go to the piano, read a speech, or do whatever you can to simulate a performance situation. Perform exactly as the person whom you have just visualized. Assume a body posture make gestures, and do anything else that mimes character. Exaggerate the motions to get a clear idea of this person's disposition. Make no judgments. Simply observe the energy you possess and the quality you express.

After the exercise write down your reactions to the experience. What did you like or dislike about this person. In your evaluation, determine if there is a subpersonality in you who is making these judgments. For example, ask yourself, "Is there a Critic in me who dislikes this person? Is someone in me afraid?" Next, ask yourself if there are qualities in this person that hinder your performance. How might you come to terms with these? Finally, see if there are qualities about this person that can help your performance. If so, what do you need to do to develop these qualities in your performance?

Keep your written notes handy for later reference during

practice. See what new insights occur as you experiment with performing as this subpersonality. After several days, repeat the exercise, this time visualizing the second subpersonality and working with it in the same way. Then for several days work with both subpersonalities. Perform first as one, then as the other. See if there are energies of one that might help the other. Find out how they might cooperate more closely.

This exercise has several ramifications. Everything visualized in it represents some part of you: the meadow, the place of the performance, as well as the persons in the audience. For most performers, the images of the audience represent some manifestation of the subpersonalities in the stagefright cluster; but they will have unique features, individual to your particular experience, and therefore may not follow the prototypes of the Critic, Doubter, or Weakling we have discussed. The stagefright part of their nature is usually revealed by their answer to what they want. The intrinsic nature of these stagefright subpersonalities, however, is disclosed or at least hinted at by the answer they give to what they need. The questions of want and need are two different issues. Wants usually come from desires, whereas needs center around such vital necessities such as compassion, acceptance, or encouragement. Further insight into their intrinsic qualities is found in the simulated performance (a very important part of the exercise) when the performer actually role plays the subpersonality. Often a surprise is in store here.

A speaker who went through this exercise saw as a member of his audience a swaggering Cynic, who made fun of the speaker's every effort. In the mock performance, however, when he walked on stage with the Cynic's swagger to present an imaginary speech, he breezed in with a nimble stride, pulsing from head to toe. The outer crust of this subpersonality was one of cynicism, but the inside core contained a soft, sinuous quality that gave the performer more buoyancy. This, in fact, was the need of the Cynic—to feel more pliant and flexible. Since the speaker in front of an audience had never allowed this to happen, the core quality surrounded itself with hard cynicism, thus becoming a main cause for stagefright.

Once in a while, an individual contacts a subpersonality who seems not to be a part of the stagefright cluster. The image may be that of a close friend, a parent, or another person who offers seeming encouragement. This subpersonality may be a Critic (possibly a Doubter or Weakling) in disguise. To make sure, ask the subpersonality, "Are you in reality my Critic (Doubter or Weakling)?" If the answer is no (and it could well be), ask, "What role do you play in my performance?" Always listen for the quality of the response. If the subpersonality offers good though conditional advice, such as, "You'll play well if you can keep your concentration," chances are good that you have contacted a subtle but powerful Critic. On the other hand, if the subpersonality speaks with genuine concern, it likely represents some quality from the other side. If this is the case, ask it, "How can you be of value in my next performance?"

Exercise 2. Dialogue with the Other Side

After you have worked for a few days with both subpersonalities in the foregoing exercise, proceed to the following one. In it, subpersonalities from the stagefright cluster begin to talk to those on the other side.

Sit in a comfortable chair (do not lie down for this, or the next exercise) and allow the body to release its tension and the mind its restless thoughts. Close your eyes and go through any steps you have found useful in previous exercises to bring the mind into quiet focus.

Recall *one* of the two subpersonalities you have been working with during the past several days. See it in your mind's eye. Ask it any question that seems appropriate. Listen to its voice tone, watch its physical gestures. What are the predominant colors of the subpersonality? How is it dressed? Look at all the characteristics of the subpersonality and find one word that describes the total quality it conveys, one word that sums up the entire substance of this subpersonality. Ponder this word a few moments. How does it sound when spoken? Listen to the distinctive tone of the word. Make no judgments. Simply listen.

As you ponder the word and listen to its tone, allow a *new* image to emerge that suggests this word. See a clear picture that conveys the meaning of this word. Give this new image a voice and allow it to speak to you. It may have a question for you, or you may have one for it. Ask the image what it wants from you; then, what it *needs* from you. Swap places with the image. In your imagination become the image and allow your body to make physical gestures that convey the substance of this image. Take the time you need to do this. Become yourself and again speak the word of the image. Listen to the sound of the word and rest a moment.

Now, find a word that expresses the exact opposite quality, one word that conveys the direct antithesis of the word you have just spoken. Listen to this contrasting word. Speak it several times and listen to the quality of its tone. Take time to hear this second word.

Allow an image to emerge that suggests this second word. Again see a clear picture of what this word expresses. Give the image a voice and ask it any question that come to mind. Swap places with this second image. As before, become the image and allow your body to make physical gestures that express this image. Become your self again and rest with your eyes closed for a few moments.

Now visualize both images. Place them in front of you at eye level. Imagine that a line between them forms the base of a triangle. As you see the images, imagine that a beam of light shines on the very top of your head. Feel its warmth as it shines down on you. Gradually let the beam of light expand so that its ray falls on the images at the base of the triangle. Watch the images as they are bathed in light. Slowly, let the images begin to move up the sides of the imaginary triangle. As they reach the top, they will converge, and a new image will be created. Make no judgments; just watch as the two images approach the top and merge into one new image.

Ponder this new image and the quality it expresses. Give the image a voice and speak to it about its value in your performance. Find one word that summarizes the quality of this image. Ask it what meaning it has in your performance. Reach out and "hold" the image in the palm of your hand. Bring your hand to your chest and symbolically draw the image into your bosom. Sense its energy; feel how it changes your body's sensations. As you become aware of your body, let it begin to move gently. Gradually become aware of your physical surroundings and in your own time, slowly open your eyes.

The meaning of the last symbol may not be clear at first. Write down your reactions. Think about the symbol. What does your Critic have to say about this symbol? Your Doubter? Your Weakling? Are you identified with one of these as you ponder its message? Consider this image in relation to those that produced it. How does it differ from the two at the base of the triangle? How do the words that describe the respective images relate? Most important, experiment with a simulated performance. Play with the energy of the first image, the second, then the third, for about two minutes apiece. After that, make changes more frequently. Finally, move rapidly from one to the other so that their energies begin to flow into one another. At a later time you can repeat the exercise, choosing to begin with the second subpersonality from exercise 1.

Exactly how the dialogue with the other side unfolds is unique to each individual. One client working with this exercise saw first a stone (that was the image that emerged from the Critic subpersonality in exercise 1), next a tree as its polar opposite, then, as the integration, the image of a burning bush. Although the analogy of the stone with the Critic was fairly obvious, the tree did not necessarily represent the direct prototype on the other side. In other words, his Critic did not make direct contact with its dual opposite—what we called the Commender—but more likely, as representative of the tree, with the Believer. Strictly labeling which subpersonality is activated on the other side, however, is unnecessary. It is enough to know that some quality in the stagefright cluster (here, the stone) contacted a quality from the other side (the tree). Together they produced the burning bush, which for this individual had special significance about the potential power his performance could achieve.

On the first experience with this exercise, it could happen initially that no voice from the other side emerges. For example, one client saw first an image he called "Thunder," and, as its opposite, one he labeled "Tinkle." Certainly these were opposites, but as it turned out, both were from the stagefright cluster: the first represented the angry power of the Critic; the second, the scared reaction of the Weakling. Nevertheless, as he moved his body around the room miming the energy of one, then the other, he began to release his pent-up anger and covered-up fear. After this energy release, gradually he saw Thunder as his rational power, firm in its resolve (here is a hint of the Mentor, albeit still influenced by the Critic); and Tinkle he saw as his feeling side, sensitive, yet playful (here is a suggestion of the Discoverer, who feels the energy of joy). Again, it is unnecessary to pigeonhole precisely which subpersonalities are revealed. Even if both originate in the stagefright cluster, it is sufficient to establish that opposites are contacted. With that, harmony becomes a possibility.

But harmony between opposites is not possible until at least some of the energy has been released; experiencing the energy is the catalyst that allows the respective qualities to transform, thereby making integration possible. Had the individual who saw Thunder and Tinkle tried to integrate these before experiencing part of their energy, his attempt probably would have failed. As it was, however, when Thunder and Tinkle were put on the imaginary triangle to climb to the top, they converged into a red crescent from which poured the sound of violins! Thus, even though this person worked with opposites within the stagefright cluster, he, by experiencing then integrating their energy, contacted a quality from the other side.

The answer we seek is found in the dichotomy of the opposites. And that is the purpose of exercise 2—to see both sides of the coin and how they relate to each other.

Exercise 3. Contacting the Higher Self

When you have gone through exercise 2 several times and have gained experience using its imagery in simulated performances, proceed to the following exercise as a means to activate energies from the Higher Self. The insights gained here are somewhat more abstract.

Sit in a comfortable chair and take a few minutes to quiet the body and rest the mind. Do this in any way that you have found best, and close your eyes. Allow an image of a meadow to emerge. Take a few moments to explore the meadow and notice if it looks any different from the ones you have seen in earlier visualizations. Remember the integrated image from exercise 2 (that which appeared at the top of the triangle) and see it now as you sit in the meadow. When you have a clear image, look around the meadow for a moment and discover in the distance a mountain. Begin to walk toward this mountain with your image.

As you approach the base of the mountain, make a choice to climb to the top, taking your image along. For climbing you may need something to help you and the image reach the top. If so, create in your mind's eye whatever you need to help you climb, and begin ascending the path. Climb easily, and in your own time find the way to the very top of the peak and sit down with your image directly in front of you.

Become aware that the sun is shining and that you can feel its warmth on the very top of your head. The sunlight also falls on the image in front of you. Just observe for a few moments.

Now, turn your eyes toward the sun and look into its glowing white light. Although the light is bright, its brilliance is soft and will not hurt your eyes. As you look into the face of the sun, discover there the image of a very old, wise person, whose eyes are full of love for you and who knows the very quintessence of who you are.

Speak to this wise person about the image you have brought with you. Ask the wise person what part this image plays in your performance. Ask any question you may have about performance and listen to the answer. This wise person may have a gift for you, one that might aid you in performance. If so, accept the gift with appreciation. See if anything else needs to be said.

When you feel complete, draw your conversation to a close and turn your eyes away from the sun. Look around the mountaintop. Rise from your place and begin to come back down, bringing with you any gift you might have received.

Find your way back to the meadow. Look around. Smell the scents of the meadow and as you do, become aware of your breathing. Slowly become aware of your physical surroundings in the room where you sit, and when you feel ready, open your eyes.

Very often this exercise yields keen insights on first experience. Performers and other creative artists seem especially inclined to benefit from this exercise, because they are aware of an inner wellspring of originality. Although such awareness may be fleeting and unpredictable, they know that from somewhere deep inside, dawn creative ideas, original thoughts, and generative insights. They perceive—more accurately, they trust—that some part of them is wiser than their usual daily nature. Trust in a Higher Self, however, need not be felt only by so-called creative persons, for regardless of one's work, creativity is a potential part of every action.

Whatever message we receive from the Higher Self, though, we need to consider its value and the meaning it holds for our performance. Sometimes—especially in the beginning stages—

a lower subpersonality may masquerade as a "wise person" (as what happened with the person who saw his German teacher). Consequently, we must use our powers of discrimination to see if in fact we have contacted our higher source of wisdom. Moreover, after we have established that, we must take an important second step. We must devise a plan of action to bring the new insight into our performance—to manifest or ground it in some way.

Grounding the message need not, in fact probably ought not, entail a complicated process. Sometimes the plan may include only the slightest adjustment in performance—a subtle change in posture, maybe a different setup on the stage. Such tiny adjustments, consciously taken, are ways in which we can "flip back" into contact with the Higher Self. They become a catalyst to stimulate energies activated previously in the guided imagery. For example, we can remember the proper pianist who always dressed in coat and tie, but who also had a fine time in a private session flailing away at a Beethoven sonata, releasing a bit of pent-up anger. At a later session when he contacted his Wise Person, he received a message quoted earlier, "Know the power within you." To him it was an electrifying perception, and for grounding this revelation, he devised a simple plan that he approached with marvelous good humor. At the next classroom recital in which he was scheduled to play, he would let out a little of his anger; he would play, as he put it, more ruggedly. To help him flip back into this attitude and conjure up a mood of ruggedness, he dressed appropriately and, for the first time in years, played with scarcely a trace of trepidation attired in a blazing western-style shirt.

Grounding our insights is the most important aspect of guided imagery. Some persons become fascinated with the images alone and delight in contacting an ever-increasing circle of subpersonalities, neglecting to ground the information. But gaining new perceptions stimulates the Higher Uncon-scious. If such forces are not utilized—if they are not carried out in operation—we risk a psychological overload in which too many ideas whirr in our heads and too few reach fruition. Therefore, rather than expanding the inner circle of subpersonalities, we need to work with those we already know (that is why they first appeared) and, as we do, to ground what we receive. In that way, they will begin to change, giving in due time new insights.

THE MATTER OF CHOICE

Applying the knowledge gained through visualization, of course, represents one aspect of choice, in that we bring into outer action certain inner perceptions. In the visualization exercises, the impetus for choice begins with the images and progresses to outward actions. But there is another side to choice wherein outward action, consciously selected, produces inner perceptions. Consequently, the impetus for choice stems from either direction—inward images or outward actions. And it is the latter we will explore in this section.

If we want to understand alternatives to stagefright, we must first enter into its disposition; then we can see more clearly what alternatives to stagefright are available. Entering into stagefright by choice, as you certainly know by now, is the main premise of this book, and we have given a number of individual accounts in support of this point. Still, the question remains: What exactly can we do to enter into stagefright willfully, and having done that, what can we do to discover other alternatives?

One suggested exercise has been designed for this purpose: to show how to choose intentionally the attitude of stagefright, then how to choose an alternative to stagefright and, in the process, how to strengthen our power of choice. The exercise extends the technique described earlier in the exercise, "Dialoguing with the Other Side." The progression in the earlier exercise moved from inward perceptions to outward actions. The progression in this exercise, however, is the reverse—from outward actions to inner mood. To further contrast, the earlier exercise was geared toward integrating opposites, whereas the main thrust of the following exercise is to affirm opposites by intentional choice. In choosing specific outward actions, we can shape our inner attitude toward performance. Here is the procedure.

Exercise 4. Strengthening the Power of Choice
Find a place where you can rehearse alone. Sit a moment and consider your performance. As precisely as you can, choose *one* aspect of your performance that causes you concern. Find one particular worry that plagues your efforts. What this might be depends on the performer. For some, the worry is about making mistakes or having memory slips; for others, it is about shaking, or having a quavering voice. Whatever the issue, concentrate on the worry. In what situation is the worry likely to occur? Who might be present? What is unique about the circumstances? When the worry comes, what happens in the body? What thoughts and feelings bubble up with the worry?

Now, in a simulated performance relive the worry. Let the worst happen. For example, make all the mistakes you can; concentrate on having a memory lapse. Exaggerate every detail so that all aspects of the worry are clearly defined. Pay particular attention to the feeling that is provoked. Exaggerate the motions associated with the feeling so that you elect to experience the feeling by choice. If you can, let the feeling expend itself. If, however, the feeling seems as though it might become overwhelming, ease away from exaggerating the energy and know that you can stop anytime you choose. Relax now and take a few deep breaths.

Think about what your performance *could* be like without this worry. If the worry were gone, what feelings would you feel? What thoughts would you think? What would the body be like? Consciously decide to shift the body into this new position—the way it would be if there were no worry. Without the worry, would you perform with more energy, more intimacy, more looseness, or what? Whatever your answer, perform in that way now. Perform as you imagine you *could* if the worry were dissolved. Act as if the worry no longer exists and begin to perform in this different way.* Stop and relax.

After going through the exercise—perhaps alternating between the two positions a few times—ask yourself these questions: What value did I find in the first position? In the second? What did I do to will the two different ways into being? How did changing my body affect my thoughts and feelings? What measures can I take in the future to will myself to perform the way I choose?

Once you have done the exercise alone, try it in front of someone else, perhaps a friend or teacher. Choose to perform with the worry, then without it. Later, try the technique in more important circumstances. But whenever you experiment in front of another person, avoid telling that person of your scheme beforehand. This activates the Weakling. It informs the other person not to expect too much because you are trying an experiment and it might fail. In effect, you are asking permission to stumble. Rather than telling others your plan, congratulate yourself inwardly for having the courage to try an experiment which might not succeed. Allowing yourself to fail is totally different from asking permission from others, because allowing yourself to fail opens up the possibility of allowing yourself to succeed.

The intent of the entire exercise is to teach us how, by choice, to disidentify from stagefright and to help us find, again by choice, a more favorable alternative. The alternative we imagine may seem at first glance to be unobtainable, but any quality that we can imagine is part of our makeup; otherwise, we could not perceive even its possibility. If we were to go through the exercise and find that the worriless positions were one of assurance, for example, we can surmise that the quality of assurance

---

*The "acting as if" concept is explained in detail by Roberto Assagioli in *The Act of Will* (Baltimore: Penguin Books, 1973), 79–84, 142–43.

lives in us, if only in a small way. We can take that tiny element and nourish it, build upon it, and in that way strengthen our power of choice to actualize it more fully.

DISTURBING THOUGHTS

My schedule was heavy—a week of workshops clustered together—and I had worked hard to prepare. On top of that, the weather was bad and I was concerned about a possible snag in my travel schedule. (Already you can hear that someone inside was revving for action.) Three days before the first workshop I started to get a case of the heebie-jeebies. "Oh no," I thought, "How can I possibly give a workshop on stagefright if I'm shaking? What kind of expert is that?"

For two days I ignored the symptoms, and thought instead of organizing my material. The symptoms smoldered and as I was getting dressed just before the first workshop, I began to shake so wildly I could hardly brush my teeth! "Wait a minute," I thought. "I need to apply to myself some of the principles I'm always talking about." With that I stopped and asked myself, "Who in there is upset?"

Immediately I knew it was my Doubter, which by this time had reached a state of alarm. I spoke to it. "Thank you for alerting me to danger. I hear your warnings and appreciate your voice. Is there anything else I should know?" I cringed, expecting the worst, but this is what it said: "Yes. Trust yourself and remember all the *good* things you're going to share with the people in the workshop."

The thought was like a wave of spring in January. I had been so preoccupied with organization that I had lost my joy and enthusiasm. But the Doubter gave it back. When I took the time to acknowledge its presence, it transformed itself into a voice from the other side.

The same transformation is likely to happen with any stagefright subpersonality when we take a moment to welcome its existence. We can use a similar approach with the other two in the cluster. The outer message of the Critic is geared toward perfectionism and sprinkled liberally with telltale directives about what we "should," "ought," "must," and "have to" do. But remember that the Critic holds at its core the quality of discernment, a quality we can begin to evoke by asking various questions related to preparation and the possibility of failure.

"What is the worst that could possibly happen if I fail?" In response to this question, one client answered, "Nothing. Then I could stop worrying about failing because I would have done it!" Admittedly, this was a fast breakthrough with his Critic and other realizations followed. Most of us do not receive such speedy insights. We generally hear something like: "You'll be laughed at," or, "You'll feel ashamed." Then, we can keep probing:

"What is the worst that could happen if I'm laughed at or feel ashamed?"

"You'll crawl under the rug."

"Then what?"

The idea is to keep questioning until you can ask yourself, "Is all this likely to happen? Do I really think my performance will be a total disaster? Is this realistic?"

Find out what is realistic. Ask yourself, "On a scale of one to ten, how well do I actually expect to perform?" What number does the Critic give? The Discerner? The Commender? Ask, "What number on the scale do I, the Objective Observer, choose? Is there anything else that needs to be done to meet that level on the scale?"

If the answer to the last question is yes, naturally find out what it is and if it is feasible for you to do. If the answer is no—there is nothing else to be done and as best you know you are prepared—then ask yourself if you are willing to accept that level of accomplishment on your next performance.

Often, however, questions posed either to the Critic or to the Doubter may be met with a string of "I don't know" responses. Every time we feel we do not know an answer, this begins the nervousness of stagefright. Still, whenever we say to ourselves, "I don't know," we can use this response as a signal, a subtle reminder that we are off-center, pulled from the Observing "I" position. Of course, we cannot know when we are on-center unless we have been off. Therefore, being off-center and knowing it is in many ways a helpful state. We can ask ourselves what we need to do to get back on. But how can we converse with a string of "I don't know" responses?

Let's take as a specific example the question above: "What do I need to do to get back on-center?" If you hear "I don't know," first recognize that the Weakling is the subpersonality that needs attention. Then try to get beyond the issue of not knowing. See what is behind the crust of ignorance by following up with such questions as these:

- "What are the things I *do* know about getting on center?"
- "What do I *imagine* the answer to be?"
- "What do I need to do to find out?"
- "What would happen if I *did* know how to get on-center? How would I be then? How would my performance be different? How would my body be? What thoughts would I think? What feelings would I feel if I *were* on-center?"
- "What is it in me that does not want me to perform from 'on-center'?"
- "Am I willing to be on-center for a few moments to see how it feels?"

Remember that any question assumes that an answer exists, even though it may not yet be available. If there is no potential answer, no question need be asked. For many of us, the problem is not in finding the answer but in formulating the question—not the unanswered question, but the one that remains unasked. One client received graphic information when he made this discovery. He suddenly realized that whenever he posed a direct question, he got a specific answer. He concluded that more important than finding the answer is asking the question. Musing on this point, he posed to himself the inevitable issue, "Just what is the question? What is it that I want to know about my performance?" And the response was, "What do I get out of stagefright? What rewards does it bring?" With that, the answers came in a flood. Having stagefright not only brought him excitement and attention, but it also made him the underdog, which in turn reduced his fear of failure. If he were the underdog, others would not expect too much of him, but rather they would be inclined to bolster his ego in an effort to soothe his stagefright. Thus they gave him the attention he craved.

Later, this individual found out he had created his own obstacles in order to gain satisfaction in overcoming them. This was how he created excitement. But he also found he could create excitement more constructively by performing with enthusiasm rather than by "conning" himself into paralyzing fear. Too, he realized he could use his performance as a means of inner nourishment, rather than as a device to squeeze out attention from others. Over a period of time, he discovered all these things in answer to his original query, "What is the question?"

The annoyance of disturbing thoughts reaches a peak in the half-hour or so before a program. This is the time when we need most stringently to disidentify with stagefright subpersonalities. All the exercises in the chapter are geared for this purpose and follow the premise that it is easier to disidentify from those things with which we have previously identified. But there are one or two other things we can do to disidentify from disturbing thoughts, especially just before a performance is scheduled to begin.

One effective means of disidentification is to switch the pronouns in the thoughts. Most of us hear the voices of stagefright as an "I" message—"I might lose face." Others hear the same voice as a "you" message. First-person pronouns usually indicate strong identification, whereas second-person pronouns suggest a lesser degree. We can deflate considerably the power of disturbing thoughts by consciously changing the pronouns to the *third person*—"My Doubter (he, she, or it) is not sure I'm ready." Changing to the third person aids in disidentifying with the thought. If the source of the thought is unclear, simply think in terms of he, she, or it, no matter what the thought. That will help clarify which subpersonality is activated, and often that awareness will be sufficient impetus to disidentify. If not, we can turn to its polar opposite and ask for a response. For example, after translating the Doubter's message into the third person, turn to the Believer (or possibly the Truster) and ask for a response. A possible reply is this: "My Believer says that I am prepared to the best of my ability at this particular time." Then ask, "With whom do I choose to identify: the Doubter or the Believer?"

The Weakling and Critic can be approached similarly by substituting the third person for "I" or "you" messages. For example, instead of thinking, "I am afraid I will fail," say, "My Weakling is afraid I will fail." Or, instead of thinking, "I must play perfectly," say, "My Critic thinks I should play perfectly."

The Critic's language can be softened if we take away the rigidity of its directives and make them more pliable. For every thought that contains "I should," "I must," or "I ought," change these to "I could," "It would be helpful," or "It would be valuable to play without mistakes"; or better, "My Critic thinks it would be valuable."

Another tactic for handling the Critic is to change negative directives into their positive equivalents. Instead of saying, "I cannot get tense," say, "I need to relax." Also, to help disidentify with the Critic, see what the Discerner or Commender can contribute. Find out what good things you have that you can share with the audience.

Keep an eye on the Weakling who says, "I don't know," "Nothing ever works," or, "Look how hard I'm trying." Determine if it is responding to the Critic or the Doubter. Check with the Risker or Discoverer. See if you are willing to risk discovering something new in your performance; determine if you are willing to enjoy yourself while you play or speak.

Finally, contact your Higher Self. Remember the earlier exercise and your conversation with the Wise Person and ask for his or her guidance. Ask this person what quality you need right now for your performance. If you received a gift in the visualization exercise, remember it now and see what meaning it has for the performance about to begin.

Most important, remember that the Wise Person sees what we have called the integral design—that composite picture of our performing conscience. Having kept this design in mind throughout all the earlier exercises, we now can call it into view more vividly to see stagefright within a larger context of reference. By our seeing this larger context, we not only disidentify from the stagefright subpersonalities, we see, paradoxically, the important function of stagefright as it fits into the integral design. Without stagefright, the integral design would cease to exist, and consequently, the higher purpose of our performance would no longer be perceivable.

Yet there is something else in this connection. Appreciating the integral design enables us to function with integrity. With this, we express ourselves with authenticity and awareness, but we also greet each performance afresh with natural spontaneity. In this natural expression, our public persona is brought into a comfortable relationship with our private self. Put another way, our *performance* reveals something of the essence of *who we are*. This is the moment performers hope to achieve.

APPENDIX

Stagefright
and Nutrition

ONCE, WHEN A CLIENT CONFESSED that she enjoyed cake and ice cream before a performance, it confirmed my guess that many performers may be unwittingly giving themselves an extra charge of stagefright by the food they eat. Although most of us were given an introduction to nutrition in grammar school, few follow through with even a basic diet because we do not understand the fundamental relationship between diet and stress. If we did, we probably would gravitate naturally to nutritious foods rather than equate "diet" with discipline and deprivation. It is true that diet alone, just as relaxation techniques by themselves, cannot eliminate the stress of stagefright. Performance stress is more an attitude, and good diet cannot change our view toward performance. Yet whereas certain foods of questionable value actually elevate stress levels, nutritious food can help us meet the stress that may already be present.

NERVES AND NUTRIENTS

In considering individual nutrients that in some way relate to "nervousness," let us keep two points in mind: the issue is many sided and our knowledge in many areas is inconclusive. Although we will focus on certain specific nutrients particularly relevant to performers, this is not to suggest that other important ones can be omitted from the diet, since the function of one often depends on the function of another.

Overall we can say that some nutrients lubricate the nervous system. Other substances heat up the nerves artificially and create a condition similar to that of a car running in neutral at full throttle. Our discussion begins with a substance capable of doing both, the one most important for the performer to understand: sugar.

SUGAR

Refined white table sugar has been stripped of all its nutrients in order to keep forever on the grocery shelf. Although refined sugar satisfies the body's need for carbohydrates, certain nutrients are needed to assimilate it as fuel. Since table sugar contains only calories and no nutrients, the various vitamins and minerals needed for sugar metabolism are leeched from other sources, producing a nutrient debt. Brown sugar fares no better, since it is nothing more than white sugar coated with a bit of molasses. Honey and molasses, counter to what many natural foods enthusiasts would have us to believe, offer little more of value than refined sugar. They do provide a few more nutrients, but not in significant amounts. All are concentrated forms of simple sugars.

When sugar is taken into the body, the pancreas is alerted to spurt up a little insulin so that the sugar can be converted to energy and the unused energy stored as fat. If the pancreas is in perfect working order, as well as the liver, which regulates the amount of sugar released into the blood, the process works beautifully. The pancreas and liver, however, may have been subjected to years of overstimulation by too much sugar or alcohol. In such a case, when a load of sugar is dumped into the system, an insulin overreaction is likely to occur. Because simple sugars are extremely concentrated, they are absorbed very rapidly. A big slug of sugar can shock even the healthiest pancreas into immediate action. Too much insulin, however, dramatically lowers blood sugar. Thus, consuming too much sugar can provoke a low-sugar response. This creates an emergency condition. An SOS is sent to the adrenal glands, which respond by sending out their juices to find more sugar. The liver is contacted to release some of its storehouse of sugar, but, in the meantime, the nerves are jangled by the adrenalin response and the "need" for sugar surfaces as a craving. Eating more sugar causes the process to be repeated. In this case, sugar is as addictive as alcohol, nicotine, or caffeine.

The problem is compounded by the fact that stagefright slows down digestion at the same time it increases the flow of adrenalin, which creates a need for sugar. In a sense, the system tugs against itself—fuel is needed, yet with the digestive process in neutral, no hunger pangs are felt. For performers in this predicament, sugar becomes their most subtle seductor. As many have found out, sugar can be speedily replaced for a short while by eating a sugar-based snack. Athletes often down a sweet "health" elixir before a strenuous game, but ingesting any "high energy" honey-based cocktail is simply the wrong thing to do metabolically. It risks a low-sugar response.

A low-sugar response can make one feel jittery, tired, hungry, and full—all at the same time. On the one hand, low blood sugar creates fatigue, sluggishness, and fuzzy thinking. On the other hand, the adrenaline response to meet the low-sugar emergency stimulates the body and thus creates a faster heartbeat, restless feelings of apprehension, and a state of insomnia. In fact, the list of symptoms associated with low blood sugar can hardly be recited in one breath: depression, anxiety, irritability, lack of concentration, forgetfulness, confusion, headache, body tremors, and cold hands and feet.

What, then, is the performer to do to insure a proper sugar level? A large part of the answer lies in complex carbohydrates. Carbohydrates are grouped in two varieties—simple and complex. Simple carbohydrates are composed of simple sugars like those already mentioned, as well as starches such as polished rice and refined flour. Complex carbohydrates include mainly *whole* grains—brown rice, whole wheat, barley, rye, etc.—and legumes—soybeans, mung beans, peas, lentils, etc. Actually, they are complex sugars and starches. They differ from simple sugars and starches in that they are constructed of many kinds of molecules, as opposed to the uniform molecular structure of simple sugars and starches, where only two or three kinds of molecules are present, since everything else has been "refined" away (except in the case of honey). Complex carbohydrates, because of the variety of their molecules, are absorbed much more slowly into the system than are simple sugars and starches. The result is a slow, steady trickle of sugar that enables balanced levels of insulin and sugar to be maintained. Some also can be stored for future use. In addition, these foods contain many other nutrients, most importantly a good supply of almost all the B-complex vitamins. These nutrients help keep glucose levels balanced and are used when sugar is metabolized.

Fructose, the sugar in many fruits, does not need insulin for digestion, and some believe this sugar will not trigger a low-sugar attack. Fructose, however, is usually found in combination with other sugars that do need insulin. Grapes, for example, are high in glucose. And, eating concentrated forms of fruit sugar such as date sugar seems unwise. Absorption is too fast because of the high concentration. Fruit juices are better diluted by an equal portion of water to slow down the absorption process, or better yet, the entire fruit should be consumed rather than just the juice. That way all the nutrients of the fruit are available and the pulp slows down absorption. Incidentally, orange pulp contains a valuable substance, rutin, not present in the juice alone.

VITAMINS

So far as is presently known, the vitamins that play the most important role in nerve functioning are the B-complex group and vitamin C, with vitamins D and E playing secondary parts. Most stress formulas contain some combination of the B vitamins and C, and both have been widely discussed as possible treatments for various nervous problems.

VITAMIN B-COMPLEX

Although we cannot say that stagefright and vitamin B-complex deficiency are directly linked, we can suggest at least an indirect connection in the fact that many symptoms of vitamin B shortages resemble various signs of stagefright. Tests show that a lack of the B vitamins can cause such things as tremors, loss of manual dexterity, lack of coordination, anxiety, depression, insomnia, forgetfulness, confusion, quick temper, and nervousness. Another close tie is revealed by evidence that suggests that worry can lower the B-complex levels. It follows, then, that certain symptoms of stagefright can be soothed in part by an adequate supply of the B vitamins.

The plan for a diet rich in B-complex is simple. It emphasizes whole grains, legumes, fresh vegetables, and some milk products. These four groups in combination afford the full gamut of B vitamins. Preventing the loss of the vitamins calls for a significant reduction—better, elimination—of sweets, alcohol, and refined or processed foods.

VITAMIN C, ASCORBIC ACID

Many nutritionists consider vitamin C to be an important ingredient in helping decrease several areas of stress: mental strain, physical overexertion, and body stress associated with diseases such as colds and flu.

The most popular source of vitamin C is citrus fruit, but all fresh fruits and most vegetables as well as sprouted grains and beans give an excellent supply. One point of interest that demonstrates the close interrelation of all nutrients is the fact that vitamin C for proper absorption needs calcium, but for the proper absorption of calcium, vitamin D is necessary. Here we have further confirmation that nature has created a splendidly balanced formula to run a delicately tuned mechanism.

MINERALS

Interrelated balance of nutrients is even more clearly evidenced when we consider stress-allied minerals. The role of calcium presents an intriguing picture for the performer. We mentioned its connection with vitamin C absorption, but its association with magnesium seems to be even more intimate. Calcium and magnesium must be balanced in a ratio of about two to one in order to function properly. Both have a tranquilizing effect and both serve nerve-impulse conduction; so it is important to keep the ratio in balance. Too little calcium in the blood can spark the nervous system and "create a case of nerves." Moreover, muscle fibers will not contract without calcium ions or, when contracted, will not release, causing cramps.

Most persons look to milk for their daily supply of calcium. Dairy products *are* high in calcium, but so are green leafy vegetables, especially mustard greens, which contain more calcium than an equal amount of milk. Green leafy vegetables also store plentiful stocks of magnesium as do beans, seeds and whole grains. Whole grains, however, lose more than 75 percent of their original magnesium when refined, and this is not added back to enriched flour or most fortified cereals.

Several other minerals vital to the body's smooth operation are collectively called trace elements since they are needed in small amounts. Long overlooked because of their minute quantities, trace elements appear to have a variety of significant functions, many of which are stress related. Still, the final verdicts are not in concerning trace elements.

The first of these elements, manganese, nourishes the nerves and coordination between nerves, brain, and muscles. Rich sources of the mineral come from the old standbys—whole grains, legumes, and green leafy vegetables. Tea, believe it or not, provides an enormous supply of manganese. One cup yields an amount equal to that found in about fifty loaves of whole wheat bread. However, tea also contains a substantial level of caffeine, and consequently it offers no solution to one who is trying to quiet backstage jitters.

Potassium and sodium form an interesting pair in the way they cause nerves to transmit impulses. Potassium is located inside the cell and sodium outside. When the nerve is stimulated, they exchange places and this exchange produces the impulse that sends a message to the brain. Too much sodium, however, pulls potassium out of the cell and, thus, artificially stimulates the nerve. Most sodium in the diet comes from table salt, which is liberally added to all processed food to prop up the taste. To counteract the stimulating influence of salt, proper balance with potassium needs to be restored. For excellent sources of potassium one can look to a large variety of fresh fruits and vegetables, especially apples, bananas, grapefruit, broccoli, spinach, and other green leafy vegetables.

Another trace element, lithium, is involved in sodium metabolism. It is available by prescription as an antidepressant. Huge doses may be toxic, but natural levels of it are found in sea vegetables such as kelp. Kelp can also be used as a salt substitute and provides a good supply of iodine, to boot.

A third pair of minerals that help support healthy nerve tissues are zinc and copper. Again, these co-workers need to be balanced. Too much copper in the system has been associated with emotional problems. Few American diets are deficient in copper, but substantial evidence suggests that zinc deficiency is widespread. Soil treated with chemical fertilizers loses perhaps half its zinc content. Zinc is needed in the makeup of the insulin molecule, and, thus, it seems likely that zinc is related to carbohydrate metabolism and in turn to energy levels. Zinc, though plentiful in whole grains and especially sprouted grains, is battered during food processing. Fresh green leafy vegetables abound in zinc. Oysters, too, offer extremely high levels, but at the expense of high cholesterol.

Chromium helps balance insulin and contains a "glucose tolerance factor" that helps keep sugar levels up. It therefore acts as a leveling influence in a low-sugar response. Liver, mushrooms, whole grains, and, particularly, nutritional yeast store valuable levels of chromium. Again, chromium like all trace elements is lost in the refining process.

One last element, chloride, is crucial to the assimilation of all minerals. Without chloride, absorption of all other minerals would be impaired as would be digestion in general. Excellent sources of chloride include kelp, dark green leafy vegetables such as chard and watercress, tomatoes, pineapple, fish, and oats.

NUTRITIONAL SUPPLEMENTS

Since nutritional supplements contain highly concentrated forms of vitamins and minerals, some people may be tempted to stock up, abetted by the American dictum that more is better. Nutritionally, such is not the case in normal circumstances. *Balance* is the byword, and supplemental vitamins and minerals tend to elevate certain nutrients artificially.

Despite that, however, supplements can and do have an appropriate place, and for the performer this usually means, obviously, before and during a strenuous performance schedule. For those who decide to use supplements, a balanced formula of nutrients is recommended, rather than concentrations of one or two. Dosages need not be large since most of them probably will be excreted anyway. In fact, large therapeutic doses of any nutrient should never be taken without professional guidance. The best means of maintaining proper nutrient levels is through a healthful diet.

THE PERFORMER'S DIET

Each of us can begin to discover the effects of a specific diet simply by "listening" to the body. For example, we can notice how we sleep after devouring a mountainous dessert at dinner, or how we feel upon polishing off a ten-ounce steak. By experimenting with foods we can see which ones make us feel better or worse. In many ways we can be our own best advisor in nourishing the body to meet stress.

In broader terms, for help in fashioning a general diet to meet the stress of stagefright, we can summarize the essential foods for a performer's diet.

The Essential Foods

A daily intake of whole grains, legumes, fresh fruits and vegetables, and some milk product will provide every nutrient we have discussed: vitamins, calcium, magnesium, manganese, potassium, zinc, chromium, lithium, chloride. Only vitamin D is in short supply and this is generously available from natural sunlight. All the rest are well represented in these four food groups. Generally speaking, and at the risk of oversimplification, we can abbreviate the predominant nutrients of each group in this way: whole grains and legumes offer vitamins B and E, fresh fruits and vegetables contain vitamin C and minerals, and milk products provide vitamin B_{12} and calcium.

Grains form the staple of the four. Those who are intolerant to wheat will want to investigate such other grains as brown rice, rye, oats, barley, and especially millet, which is a veritable storehouse of many nutrients, including complete proteins. Delicious breads can be baked substituting other whole-grain flours and even some bean flours for the usual wheat base.

Legumes complement grains and comprise a varied list of

wholesome foods: mung beans, split peas, kidney beans, lentils, etc. Nutritionally the list is headed by soybeans. These have a pungent taste to which some object. This taste is not found in two soybean products, miso and tofu, which are extremely rich in nutrients. Miso is similar to soy sauce, another fine food if it has not been doctored with commercial additives. Both grains and legumes should be cooked well to insure proper absorption by the body.

Most fresh vegetables, on the other hand, are more nutritious when eaten raw or only lightly cooked. The fresher they are, the more nutrients they retain. Dark green leafy vegetables, such as chard, kale, collards, and mustard greens, need to be emphasized since all are good sources of folic acid, calcium, magnesium, and zinc.

For the performer whose stomach is upset by the lactose in milk, soured skimmed milk products—yogurt, buttermilk, whey—are easily digested. Avoid pasteurized commercial yogurt (especially that with added fruit preserves, which are loaded with sugar). Pasteurization kills the yogurt culture, the whole point of yogurt's value. Cheese is hard to digest and produces mucus in the body, as does milk. Some persons, therefore, may want to avoid both, for example singers and speakers who need a phlegm-free throat.

Those who wish to eat other animal protein can choose from baked chicken or fish and perhaps an occasional serving of liver. These make much better choices than fatty hamburgers and steaks. Animal fat is hard to digest, high in cholesterol, and it draws oxygen from body tissues.

Fresh and unprocessed foods are by far recommended over refined, packaged foods, most of which contain salt, artificial coloring, sugar, chemical preservatives, and threadbare nutrients.

Stagefright and Digestion

Stagefright slows down digestion and makes the digestive tract particularly susceptible to alien elements. For this reason the system should not be taxed on performance day with large meals or foods to which the body is unaccustomed. It is better to rely on a backlog of nutritious meals rather than attempt to cram in all the nutrients at the last minute. Cramming will not work anyway, despite the dedication of some to last-minute remedies. The body needs at least twelve to fourteen days before dietary improvements can be effected. If stress levels are high, one should avoid eating anything but a healthful snack three or four hours before the event. Unfamiliar foods and foods to which one has an intolerance should, of course, be avoided.

Food and Energy

Some performers look to protein to provide energy, and insist on devouring a big steak on the day of performance. Again, digesting animal fat draws oxygen from body tissues, the reason that one gets sleepy after a heavy meal. Consistent high-energy levels, though related to protein intake, are directly determined by steady optimum blood-sugar levels, and this depends mainly on complex carbohydrates, not protein. Moreover, the most important complex carbohydrates—whole grains and legumes— yield in combination a complete protein rivaling that of meat and without high cholesterol or excessive oxygen consumption from body tissue.

To keep sugar levels, and in turn energy levels, at a stable maximum, here in capsule form are highlights from earlier suggestions.

1. Emphasize complex carbohydrates—whole grains, most legumes, potatoes, and bananas.
2. Reduce or eliminate simple starches and sugars—white flour, honey, molasses, and white sugar (see below).
3. Emphasize foods rich in vitamin B—whole grains, legumes, lecithin, nutritional yeast, dark green leafy vegetables, and sour milk products. (Although eggs and liver are rich sources of B vitamins, both are high also in cholesterol and, there-

fore, should be used with discretion.) This list of foods contains not only the other sugar-balancing nutrients, vitamins C and E, zinc chromium, manganese, and potassium, but also *all* the stress-related nutrients we have covered.

4. Rely on *whole* fruits (except grapes, which are high in glucose) to satisfy a sweet tooth. Include these in a light snack before performance.

5. Avoid alcohol, nicotine, caffeine, and sugar in all forms. In many ways these are killers for the performer:
   a. All stimulate the adrenal glands.
   b. All confuse sugar metabolism and run the risk of creating a low-sugar response. Because they do so, all potentially can become addictive physiologically and psychologically.
   c. Caffeine found in coffee, tea, and chocolate destroys digestive enzymes.
   d. Cigarette smoke consumes vitamin C.
   e. Alcohol and sugar leech B vitamins from the system.

Some may object to these ideas as too stringent and wonder if certain favorite delights are never to be enjoyed again. Is ice cream, for example, forever to be relegated to the realm of sin? Not always. We can enjoy all food, even occasional "infractions." Make changes gradually. Rigidity, even in diet, rarely pays dividends. Pay attention to the foods that are healthful rather than concentrating sternly on items that need to be avoided. Eat leisurely, tasting each bite. Most important, know the effect of food on the body and see how it prepares the "instrument" for the fun of performance. In this way we will move naturally toward a healthful diet to help meet the stress of stagefright.

FURTHER READING ON NUTRITION

Airola, Paavo. *How to Get Well: Dr. Airola's Handbook of Natural Healing*. Phoenix: Health Plus Publishers, 1974.

Ballentine, Rudolph. *Diet and Nutrition: A Holistic Approach.* Honesdale, Pa.: Himalayan International Institute, 1976.

Brewster, Letitia, and Jacobson, Michael. *The Changing American Diet.* Washington: Center for Science in the Public Interest, 1978.

Bricklin, Mark. *The Practical Encyclopedia of Natural Healing.* Emmaus, Pa.: Rodale Press, 1976.

Cheraskin, E.; Ringsdorf, W. M., Jr.; and Clark, James W. *Diet and Disease.* New Canaan, Conn.: Keats Publishing, 1977.

Cheraskin, E.; Ringsdorf, W. M., Jr.; and Brecher, Arline. *Psychodietetics: Food as the Key to Emotional Health.* New York: Stein and Day, 1974.

INDEX